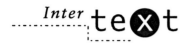

The Language of Humour

This accessible satellite textbook in the Routledge INTERTEXT series is unique in offering students hands-on, practical experience of textual analysis focused on the language of humour. Written in a clear, user-friendly style by a practising teacher, it combines practical activities with texts, followed by commentaries to show how messages are constructed from language and suggestions for further activities. It can be used individually or in conjunction with the series core textbook, *Working with Texts: A core book for language analysis.*

Aimed at A-Level and beginning undergraduate students, *The Language of Humour*:

- examines the ways that humour is created in both spoken and written language;
- explores the relationship between humour and social attitudes; the status of the targets of humour, the joke tellers and the audience;
- focuses on the social aspects of humour, and asks what it contributes to current debates on 'political correctness' and censorship;
- analyses a rich variety of humorous text examples, from the classics of Charles Dickens and Oscar Wilde to the contemporary sketches of French and Saunders, Eddie Izzard, Victoria Wood, Reeves and Mortimer, the cartoons of Gary Larson, and the sitcom *Friends*.

Alison Ross is a visiting lecturer at Leeds University and Sheffield Hallam University. She is a senior examiner and moderator for the NEAB English Language A Level.

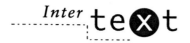

The Intertext series

◎   Why does the phrase 'spinning a yarn' refer both to using language and making cloth?

◎   What might a piece of literary writing have in common with an advert or a note from the milkman?

◎   What aspects of language are important to understand when analysing texts?

The Routledge INTERTEXT series will develop readers' understanding of how texts work. It does this by showing some of the designs and patterns in the language from which they are made, by placing texts within the contexts in which they occur, and by exploring relationships between them.

The series consists of a foundation text, *Working with Texts: A core book for language analysis*, which looks at language aspects essential for the analysis of texts, and a range of satellite texts. These apply aspects of language to a particular topic area in more detail. They complement the core text and can also be used alone, providing the user has the foundation skills furnished by the core text.

Benefits of using this series:

◎   **Unique** – written by a team of respected teachers and practitioners whose ideas and activities have also been trialled independently

◎   **Multi-disciplinary** – provides a foundation for the analysis of texts, supporting students who want to achieve a detailed focus on language

◎   **Accessible** – no previous knowledge of language analysis is assumed, just an interest in language use

◎   **Comprehensive** – wide coverage of different genres: literary texts, notes, memos, signs, advertisements, leaflets, speeches, conversation

◎   **Student-friendly** – contains suggestions for further reading; activities relating to texts studied; commentaries after activities; key terms highlighted and an index of terms

The series editors:

Ronald Carter is Professor of Modern English Language in the Department of English Studies at the University of Nottingham and is the editor of the Routledge INTERFACE series in Language and Literary Studies. He is also co-author of *The Routledge History of Literature in English*. From 1989 to 1992 he was seconded as National Director for the Language in the National Curriculum (LINC) project, directing a £21.4 million in-service teacher education programme.

Angela Goddard is Senior Lecturer in Language at the Centre for Human Communication, Manchester Metropolitan University, and was Chief Moderator for the project element of English Language A Level for the Northern Examination and Assessment Board (NEAB) from 1983 to 1995. Her publications include *The Language Awareness Project: Language and Gender*, vols I and II, 1988, and *Researching Language*, 1993 (Framework Press).

First series title:

Working with Texts: A core book for language analysis
Ronald Carter, Angela Goddard, Danuta Reah, Keith Sanger, Maggie Bowring

Satellite titles:

The Language of Sport
Adrian Beard

The Language of Newspapers
Danuta Reah

The Language of Advertising: Written texts
Angela Goddard

The Language of Humour
Alison Ross

The Language of Poetry
John McRae

The Language of Fiction
Keith Sanger

Related titles:

INTERFACE series:

Language, Literature and Critical Practice
David Birch

Literary Studies in Action
Alan Durant and Nigel Fabb

A Linguistic History of English Poetry
Richard Bradford

Dramatic Discourse
Vimala Herman

The Routledge History of Literature in English: Britain and Ireland
Ronald Carter and John McRae

English in Speech and Writing
Rebecca Hughes

The Language of Jokes
Delia Chiaro

Feminist Stylistics
Sara Mills

The Discourse of Advertising
Guy Cook

Language in Popular Fiction
Walter Nash

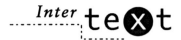

The Language of Humour

- Alison Ross

London and New York

First published 1998
by Routledge
2 Park Square, Milton Park, Abingdon,
Oxon, OX14 4RN

Simultaneously published in the USA and
Canada
by Routledge
270 Madison Ave, New York NY 10016

Reprinted 1999

Transferred to Digital Printing 2005

*Routledge is an imprint of the
Taylor & Francis Group*

© 1998 Alison Ross

Typeset in Stone Sans/Stone Serif by
Solidus (Bristol) Limited

*British Library Cataloguing in Publication
Data*

A catalogue record for this book is
available from the British Library

*Library of Congress Cataloguing in Publication
Data*

Ross, Alison, 1949–
   The language of humour/Alison Ross.
      p. cm. – (Intertext)
   Includes bibliographical references.
   ISBN 0–415–16912–7 (pb)
   1. English wit and humor – History and
criticism. 2. English language – Style.
3. Style, Literary. 4. Comic, The.
I. Title. II. Series: Intertext (London,
England)
PR931.R67   1998
827.009–dc21
                                           97–24610
                                                  CIP

ISBN 0–415–16912–7

contents

acknowledgements

Thanks to the many friends, colleagues and students who gave me their favourite jokes on scraps of paper or even sent me books and videos, while I was writing the book. Particular thanks to my sons, Jonathan and Alastair Gregory, who tried to keep me up-to-date with current trends in humour.

The following texts have been reprinted by courtesy of the copyright holders:

1   Excerpt from 'What time is it Eccles?' from *The Goon Show*, written by, and by permission of Spike Milligan
2   Extract from the Parrot sketch by permission of Python Productions Ltd
3   'Slow it right down' by Sophie Hannah taken from *Hotels Like Houses*, by permission of Carcanet Press Ltd, 1996
4   'Handbag' and 'Interior Design' by Neil Gauckwin, by permission of Neil Gauckwin
5   'Bronteburgers' and 'He Didn't' taken from *Chunky* by Victoria Wood, Methuen, 1996, by permission of Victoria Wood
6   'Record Choice' and 'Fat Aristocrats' by French and Saunders taken from *A Feast of French and Saunders*, Heineman, 1991, by permission of French and Saunders
7   'A Letter From Helen of Troy' by Adèle Geras, previously published by Rockingham Press in *Voices in the Doll's House*, by permission of Rockingham Press
8   Extract from *Interview with Clive Anderson* by Peter Cook by permission of David Higham Associates Ltd
9   The Far Side by Gary Larson © Farworks, Inc. Used with permission. All rights reserved

The publishers have made every effort to contact copyright holders although this has not been possible in some cases. Outstanding permission will be remedied in future editions. Please contact Moira Taylor at Routledge.

introduction

Humour has a high profile in our society. A glance through the television guides will show this: sitcoms and comedy shows are on prime-time television every evening. In January 1997 the final episode of the sitcom, *Only Fools and Horses* was watched by a record number of 24.5 million viewers. Humorous books are usually in the bestseller lists: in January 1997 the best-selling paperback was *Notes from a Small Island* by Bill Bryson, and another five humorous books were in the top twenty. Comedians like Eddie Izzard, Victoria Wood, Jo Brand, Lennie Henry can fill venues as well as top bands. These are all examples of mass media, but humour has a fashionable status even at a personal level: most advertisements in the lonely hearts columns refer to a GSOH (they don't even have to spell out a Good Sense Of Humour). Few people today would own up to a lack of humour.

Humour is influential – from political satire to joking as a way of establishing friendships and excluding others. The examples included in this book all made someone laugh at some time, but the context for humour is a crucial element. This means that a book *about* humour is unlikely to be funny. What it offers is an examination of the ways that humour is created in language. While this may spoil the immediate gut reaction of laughter, it is important to understand how the response of laughter is triggered.

Unit 1 moves towards a definition of what counts as 'humour' and asks you to consider the factors which combine to make you laugh. Then three theories of humour are examined in turn. One theory states that we laugh at the unexpected or incongruous. Unit 2 looks at types of ambiguity, from individual words to the structure of English sentences. These types of double meanings are what many people think of as humour, but there are more subtle ways in which the humorist jolts us into laughter, by breaking the normal expectations of language in use. These language conventions are examined in Unit 3. The next two units move on to the *subject* of the humour. The superiority theory explains our tendency to laugh when someone we despise is the target. Seeing which groups are the targets of humour can give a snapshot of that society's attitudes. Unit 4 looks at the ways in which these attitudes are established or challenged by language use, and the ways in which the response is affected by the stance of the joke-teller or the audience. The psychic release theory explains laughter as caused by the sense of a taboo being broken. The focus in Unit 5 is not on the reason *why* certain areas are taboos but on which areas are considered 'unspeakable' and *how* the humour is created – through either taboo words or innuendo. The remaining three units examine texts from the genres of literature, radio, television and stand-up comedy. Since much humour is a matter of personal taste, and contemporary humour may have a short 'shelf-life', the texts are there to represent a range of examples and indicate ways of investigating them. The aim of the book is to outline a framework of analysis that can be applied to any humour in speech or writing. It was a challenge to say anything revealing about the strangest, and funniest, examples from the 1990s: Vic Reeves and Bob Mortimer on television, the cartoons of Gary Larson and the stand-up comedy of Eddie Izzard. By the year 2000 there will be new humour which is equally tricky to analyse. This is the essence of humour: surprise, innovation and rule-breaking.

'Just for a laugh?'

What is humour?

One definition of humour is: 'something that makes a person laugh or smile'. Like all straightforward definitions, exceptions can be found. It's possible to claim that something is humorous, even though no one laughed at the time - and it can often happen that people laugh, but someone can claim, 'That's not funny'. Smiling and laughter can also be a sign of fear or embarrassment. Despite these objections, the *response* is an important factor in counting something as humour. Examining the language can then help to explain *why* people laugh.

When does laughter occur?

People laugh in company. Research has shown that when people are alone they rarely laugh, even though the same example of humour makes them do so in a room full of people. There is a strong social aspect to the way people respond to humour. If you watch your favourite comedy in the presence of people who remain straight-faced, it can stop you finding it so funny. Because it's important to sense other people responding to humour, 'canned laughter' is used for television or radio comedy. The same joke can work brilliantly in one context and die in another, as stand-up comedians find, travelling from one venue to

1

another. Like other aspects of language, humour is a way in which people show their allegiance to a group. If someone signals their intention to say something humorous, the listeners are immediately ready to laugh. People often laugh when given this sort of cue, regardless of whether they even got the joke.

The opposite happens if the listeners want to distance themselves from the speaker. Once you feel that someone is old-fashioned, silly or racist, for example, you are unlikely to laugh. The social context is important for the creation and reception of humour. It is hard for humour to cross boundaries of time and social groups – humour becomes outdated as quickly as fashion, and is often dependent on particular cultures and attitudes. There are other ways in which the context is important. The phrase 'There's a time and a place for everything' is true of humour. It is not felt to be appropriate in certain situations, for example if it seems trivial or is a distraction from serious matters. It's also difficult to take humour 'cold'. Few people laugh first thing in the morning, so broadcast comedy programmes are scheduled for the relaxing parts of the day. Even when a comedy event happens in the evening, warm-up artists are often used to get audiences in the right mood.

'Just for a laugh?'

Humour has various effects, whether these are intentional or not. It is simplistic to say that it's just for a laugh. It's possible to laugh and admit that, in a sense, it's not funny. There may be a target for the humour – a person, an institution or a set of beliefs – where the underlying purpose is deadly serious. Humour can occur in surprisingly serious contexts, as in sick jokes about death.

So, although laughter is not a necessary or sufficient condition of humour, from a commonsense point of view it's a useful starting point for a definition.

Humour may be thought of as a peripheral, leisure activity which lacks the more obvious significance of literature, advertising and the media. Having a good time with friends usually involves having a laugh. But what makes us laugh and why?

Activity with text

How do you respond to the following jokes? Because they are listed in a book about humour, they are out of their usual context. Even so, group them in order of preference. For those low down on your list, comment on the situation in which they *could* be funny — who might be telling the joke, where, when and to whom? Are there some you would consider *not* funny in any possible situation?

1 'Do you believe in clubs for young people?' 'Only when kindness fails.' (W.C. Fields)
2 Why do women have small feet? So they can get closer to the sink.
3 What's the difference between a bad marksman and a constipated owl? One shoots but can't hit.
4 If Noel Edmunds, Stalin and Hitler were in a room and you had only two bullets in your gun, who do you shoot? Noel Edmunds - twice.
5 What's orange and sounds like a parrot? A carrot.
6 Why does Edward Woodward have 4 D's in his name? Because if he didn't he'd be called E-war Woo-war-.
7 I have an existential map. It has 'You are here' written all over it.
8 God is not dead but alive and well and working on a much more ambitious project.
9 Winter is nature's way of saying 'Up yours.'
10 Weather forecast for tonight: dark.
11 There is no gravity. The earth sucks.
12 When the going gets tough, the tough go shopping
13 One hundred thousand lemmings can't be wrong.
14 Did you hear the one about the man who walked into a bar and said 'Ouch!'?
15 LOVE, n. A temporary insanity curable by marriage.
16 MAD, adj. Affected with a high degree of intellectual independence.
17 Fox hunting is the unspeakable in pursuit of the inedible. (Oscar Wilde)
18 Two cows in a field. One says, 'Moo.' Other says, 'You bastard, I was going to say that.'
19 Two cows in a field. One says 'Are you worried about this BSE scare?' 'Of course not, I'm a helicopter.'
20 Man in a bar: 'I just got a bottle of gin for my mother-in-law.' Second man: 'Sounds like a good swap.'

Commentary

Personal taste is a crucial aspect of humour, so it is unlikely that any two people will coincide in their ranking of the jokes. Your taste in humour will also change over time: certain styles seem outdated once you have heard that sort of joke too often. It also changes less predictably with mood, even the time of day. However you may be able to identify a type and style of humour that you tend to appreciate. If you enjoy wordplay and puns, numbers 1, 11 and 20 in the list have an element of ambiguity, though you may feel that the wordplay is corny or trivial. Some jokes have an element of shock, because taboo subjects or words are mentioned (3, 18) or because they attack a target (2, 4, 20). Your reaction will depend partly on your attitude to the subject – you might object to jokes about women or feel offended by cruelty or crudity in humour. Others make some neat witticism about human nature and society (15, 16, 17). You are more likely to respond to the clever use of language if you share the attitude of the joke-teller. Some allude to a familiar saying and twist it (8, 9, 12, 13). This type of cross-reference needs to be both understood and appreciated in its new use. Others refer to the actual conventions of humour and joking and subvert them (5, 6, 14). There is an element of irony and detachment in jokes about jokes. Enjoyment of the surreal leads to a bizarrely unexpected notion (7, 18, 19) rather than a surprising punchline. Many examples of humour do several of these things at the same time (1, 20). Others make us laugh although it is hard to explain why. Number 10 is stating the obvious, so it's odd as a forecast – but, then again, weather forecasts often do state the obvious, so perhaps it's a comment on that.

Extension

Collect examples of humour that you enjoy. Also list those that you do not find funny at all. You may find examples from fields such as advertising or newspaper headlines, as well as texts clearly intended as comedy. Attempt a broad characterisation into types of humour, using some of the categories mentioned above: wordplay and ambiguity, taboo-breaking, attacking a target, **allusion** and **intertextuality**, nonsense or the absurd. These features will be discussed in more detail in the next four units. Are there some examples which do not fall into these categories? If so, try to describe the source of humour.

Bear the following in mind when selecting texts for your own project work or investigation.

Visual humour – as in silent films, cartoons and clowning – is outside the scope of this book, though it is possible to comment on the way cartoon captions interact with visuals to create humour. Some spoken humour, particularly of impressionists like Rory Bremner, relies so much on features like the quality and tone of voice that it would need a sophisticated phonetic analysis – also outside the book's scope. Use the following as a guide to choosing texts that are suitable for language analysis:

◎ The humour must be verbal – either written or spoken.
◎ It will generally be intentional, though perhaps based on inadvertent slips of the tongue.
◎ Your response must be to aspects of language.
◎ Those aspects should be diverse enough to allow extended comment.

'I say, I say, I say'

The incongruity theory

The *context* for humour is crucial for determining whether an individual finds something amusing or not. Even so, it is possible to examine the features of language that have the potential to make people laugh. The incongruity theory focuses on the element of surprise. It states that humour is created out of a conflict between what is expected and what actually occurs in the joke. This accounts for the most obvious feature of much humour: an ambiguity, or double meaning, which deliberately misleads the audience, followed by a punchline.

> 'Do you believe in clubs for young people?'
> 'Only when kindness fails.'
>
> (W. C. Fields)

It is reasonable to understand the word 'clubs' in the sense of 'leisure groups', but the punchline shows that it was referring to 'weapons'.

A dictionary definition of **incongruous** is: 'inconsistent; not fitting well together; disjointed; unsuitable', which all sound like negative terms. Unintentional humour may well be caused by some lapse in expression, but deliberate humour is carefully planned, often to the exact wording and timing. In *The Cambridge Encyclopedia of Language* (Crystal 1987) David Crystal comments: 'variations in self-expression are most noticeable in those areas of language use where great care is being taken, such as literature and humour.' The *lapse* - in the previous example - happens on the part of the tellee, who has failed to grasp the intended sense. In this way humour breaks an important rule of language use: that we should try to communicate as clearly as possible. (Unit 3 looks at the ways in which the 'co-operative principle' can be flouted.) The examples of humour in this unit use the possibilities for **ambiguity** in the words or structure of language.

This type of humour is often a one-off joke or a 'gag' occurring in extended texts. In such small examples of humour the term *incongruity* refers to the possibility for two meanings being understood from the utterance. This is often called a **pun**. The humour will often have the following elements:

◎ There is a conflict between what is expected and what actually occurs in the joke.
◎ The conflict is caused by an ambiguity at some level of language.
◎ The punchline is surprising, as it is not the expected interpretation, but it resolves the conflict: 'Have you got a light, Mac?' 'No, but I've got a dark brown overcoat.'

The reason for not finding such a joke funny might be that you don't perceive the ambiguity. Or it might be because the double meaning is laboured or corny: you acknowledge that it's a joke, but not a funny one.

Structural ambiguity

This unit looks at examples of **structural ambiguity**. This can occur in the English language at various levels:

◎ **phonology** - the sounds that make up the language
◎ **graphology** - the way the language is represented in written form
◎ **morphology** - the way words themselves are structured
◎ **lexis** - the individual words of the language
◎ **syntax** - the way the words are structured into phrases, clauses and sentences.

In the joke quoted above, there is an ambiguity at the level of lexis and phonology, as there are two possible meanings for each of the words 'light' and 'Mac/mac'. There is also an ambiguity in syntax: the listener interprets the structure as finishing on the noun 'light', with the name of the person added on. The punchline shows that 'light mac' should be regarded as an adjective + noun unit.

However, it is difficult to find examples of humour which do not also involve conventions about language as a social act. The second speaker is being deliberately awkward here: no one approaches a stranger with an enquiry about the contents of their wardrobe. The term **discourse** will be used for stretches of language longer than the sentence, in particular the ways that conversation works. Once people are involved in discourse, it is not enough to be able to structure the language in the right form, they must also understand conventions about what is appropriate to say in various situations. For example, in a sketch involving a doctor and a patient, the doctor concludes the interview by saying 'If you have any further worries, don't hesitate to ask.' The patient leans forward anxiously and says 'If the universe is expanding all the time, where does it all go?' Here it is a matter not of misinterpreting the meaning of the word 'worries' but of knowing the sort of worries that a doctor deals with. (Unit 3 looks at incongruity in language use.)

Phonology

Many jokes are based on the fact that there can be two possible interpretations of the same group of sounds. One of the earliest riddles which children hear and tell is:

What's black and white and red/read all over? A newspaper.

The term **homophone** refers to words that are pronounced the same but spelt differently: for example, 'saw', 'sore'. The possibility for confusion can happen only in spoken language, as the two words look quite distinct when written down. (These are distinct from **homonyms**, which are identical in spelling and pronunciation, but have a different meaning. For example, 'saw' meaning looked at, and 'saw' meaning a tool for cutting wood.) There are many homophones in the English language, because the English system of spelling is not based on representing each sound or phoneme with a distinct letter or symbol. Sometimes there is just a similarity of sound.

Headline: Cloning Around

Here the set phrase 'Clowning [/kləʊnɪŋ/] around' is altered by using a word of slightly different sound, /klaʊnɪŋ/.

It is possible to find many potential ambiguities because of the way

9

that English vowel sounds, in particular, are pronounced in connected speech. Unlike a language like Italian, unstressed syllables in English tend to reduce the vowel sound to a schwa /ə/. It is hardly surprising that there is confusion about how to spell words, because all vowel *letters* can be spoken as /ə/, for example in the mistake on a driving school advert: 'Duel control cars'. Both 'dual' and 'duel' are pronounced /djuəl/, even when the word is spoken in isolation. The schwa sound occurs often in the unstressed words once words are spoken as part of an utterance: 'Are you going to the shops?' could easily be pronounced /ə jə gəuɪŋ tə ðə ʃɒps/, with five schwa sounds.

In spoken English, ambiguities can be caused by the way that words are stressed and by their intonation: 'It's not my hand you should kiss' (Voltaire, *Candide*). Using contrastive stress on either '*my* hand' or 'my *hand*' would radically change the meaning. Notice which syllables are given primary stress to distinguish the meanings of these examples:

'convict (noun)	con'vict (verb)
a dark 'room	a 'darkroom (where photos are developed)

There is a slight difference in **stress** and **intonation** that could resolve the ambiguity in the following joke.

'How do you make a cat drink?'
'Easy, put it in the liquidiser.'

cat 'drink = drink for a cat (like 'dark room')
'cat drink = drink out of a cat (like 'darkroom')

The change in stress indicates different structures – two separate words or a compound word.

In spoken language individual words are run together. Only the context tells the listener how the stream of sounds should be divided: 'Some others I've seen' versus 'Some mothers I've seen'. Sequences of popular joke formulas exploit this type of ambiguity:

'Knock, knock.'
'Who's there?'
'Noah.'
'Noah who?'
'Noah good place to eat?'

Keep Fit by Jim Nastics

Victorian Transport by Orson Cart

Unintentional humour can be created in spontaneous speech. Mrs Malaprop is a character in Sheridan's play *The Rivals*, who doesn't quite get words right and uses ones of a similar sound but an inappropriate meaning. This is now termed a **malapropism**:

Illiterate him, I say, quite from your memory.

This is sometimes the cause of accidental 'howlers' found in students' work and collected by teachers and examiners: 'The girl tumbled down the stairs and lay *prostitute* at the bottom.'

The Reverend William Archibald Spooner was a tutor at Oxford University who became famous for mixing up the initial sounds of words (a device now called **Spoonerism**), although many of the examples attributed to him are now known to be apocryphal (invented). Here he is addressing a student:

You have tasted two worms and must leave by the town drain.

Such a device can also be used deliberately for humour, as in the following, which suggests – but does not articulate – a taboo word:

He is a shining wit.

Allusions in humour involve extra-linguistic knowledge, in other words knowledge about the world. The double meaning may involve reference to a saying or quotation. If the listener does not share the same awareness of this, the ambiguity cannot be recognised.

Cogito ergo Boom. (Susan Sontag)

The listener needs to know the French philosopher Descartes's statement 'Cogito ergo sum' (I think, therefore I am) and also to understand that 'Boom' refers to a nuclear explosion.

Activity with text

Categorise the following jokes under the types given above. Indicate where the ambiguity occurs, by underlining, or marking stress etc. Note those where recognition of an allusion is required.

1 And the batsman's Holding, the bowler's Willie. (cricket commentator Brian Johnstone)
2 She's the kind of girl who climbed the ladder of success, wrong by wrong. (Mae West)
3 Manchester children all follow United, because their mothers tell them to stay away from the Maine Road.
4 Macho does not prove mucho. (Zsa Zsa Gabor)
5 Be alert. (*Civil Defence poster with added graffiti*) Your country needs lerts.
6 Never darken my Dior again. (Beatrice Lillie)
7 (*Dorothy Parker, when challenged to use the word 'horticulture' in a sentence*) You can lead a horticulture, but you can't make her think.
8 Je t'adore. (*caption on front of greeting card*) Inside: Shut it yourself, you lazy git.
9 Stop Miss World – we want to get off. (*banner*)
10 Man walks into a bar and orders a pint of jelly and some roof tiles. He belongs to the Campaign for Surreal Ale.

Commentary

Extra-linguistic knowledge is needed in 1, 2, 3, 6, 7, 9 and 10, which allude either to proper names referring to specific people, places and organisations (cricketers named Holding and Willie, Maine Road as the home of Manchester City football ground; Christian Dior as the name of a fashion designer; the Campaign for Real Ale organisation) or to well-known sayings ('to climb the ladder of success, rung by rung'; 'Never darken my door again'; 'You can lead a horse to water, but you can't make it drink'; 'Stop the world – we want to get off'). 1 and 3 are exact homophones, whereas 2, 4, 6, 8, 9 and 10 rely on similarity of sound. 1 relies on sentence stress and 5, 7 and 8 on word boundaries.

Graphology

Graphology refers to the way in which the language is represented visually. Some examples of humour need to be seen rather than heard. Although short verbal jokes often found as graffiti can also work when they are spoken, sometimes the appearance of letters and words can imitate their sense, as in the following example:

Yo-Yos rule O

-

-

-

      K

The notion of a running gag takes a particular known formula and makes a series of variations on it, so it is essential to be aware of the original formula, in this case: x rules OK.

Dyslexia lures KO

Amnesia rules O

Adding or changing the lettering of signs is a casual form of wordplay, perhaps childish, as in the following examples.

TO LET – TOILET

BROOM CLOSE + T (*on a street sign*)

The archetypal bad boy cartoon character, Bart Simpson, re-arranges the words on a display menu, changing COD PLATTER to COLD PET RAT.

Forming **anagrams** from well-known names can sometimes provide delightfully incongruous yet apt reformulations; or witty variations on familiar sayings.

Tony Blair, a PM = I'm a Tory, Plan B

Virginia Bottomley = I'm an evil Tory bigot

Bad spellers of the world untie

Like the ambiguity of **word boundaries** in spoken language, the physical spaces between words can be blurred in written language to provide ambiguities of meaning, as in the following printed in capitals on a postcard.

THE PEN IS
MIGHTIER THAN
THE PENIS

There are accidental howlers caused by misspelling, collected by teachers and displayed for general amusement: 'They lived in huts and

13

there was rush mating on the floor.' The 'Lost Consonants' series of cartoons in the *Guardian* (by Graham Rawle) relies on the pleasure of seeing how the omission of a single letter can create absurd new meanings.

It would ruin his career if the sandal hit the headlines.

Andrew Lloyd-Webber writes another hit musical!

Acronyms are words formed from the initial letters of other words. They are so common today - organisations try to find a catchy title that will stick in the mind - that this tendency itself is mocked in the following comments.

What we need to use is courtesy, respect and patience - CRAP. (*Brittas Empire*)

'I think there are too many TLA's.'
'What's a TLA?'
'A Three Letter Abbreviation.'

Activity

Collect examples of written humour which depend on the visual representation of the language. Group them into categories.

Morphology

Morphology refers to the way that individual words are formed. A **morpheme** is the smallest meaningful unit of sense. Many words are simply made up of a single morpheme and cannot be split down into smaller parts, for example 'table'. Other words are clearly more complex and formed from a number of units, for example 'antidisestablish-mentarianism', which has the **prefixes** 'anti-' and 'dis-' and the **suffixes** '-ment', '-arian' and '-ism'. People's instinctive knowledge of the ways that morphemes are used to form meanings can be exploited in jokes which point out the possible ambiguities.

The same sound, or the same group of letters, can be a word or a **bound morpheme** (prefix or suffix) or a syllable, depending on the context. Think, for example, of the different morphological structure of the words 'childhood' and 'rainhood', where 'hood' is a suffix meaning 'state' in the first case, but a free morpheme meaning 'covering for the head' in the second. Or words like 'slowish' where '-ish' is a suffix indicating the sense of 'slightly', yet '-ish' is not a suffix in the word 'establish'. This potential confusion creates the following joke:

'What's a baby pig called?'
'A piglet.'
'So what's a baby toy called?'
'A toilet.'

'-let' can often be a suffix meaning small. Sometimes it occurs just as the final syllable in a word. In this case the French word 'toilette' is the diminutive of 'toile', the word for 'cloth', not 'toy'.

The following witty definition is based partly on a phonological similarity between the prefix 'mis-' and the word 'miss'; a prefix is interpreted as a free morpheme in a compound word.

MISFORTUNE, n. The kind of fortune that never misses. (Ambrose Bierce, *The Devil's Dictionary*)

Compound words are formed from two free morphemes. The order is significant; they can't be reversed without altering the meaning: for example an 'overpass' is not the same as 'Passover'.

I should have been a country-western singer. After all, I'm older than most western countries. (George Burns)

The meaning is also difficult to explain simply by referring to the constituent parts.

Have you heard the one about the man who bought a paper shop? It blew away.

'Paper shop' can mean either 'shop made out of papers' or 'shop that sells papers'. Logically, you might expect the meaning of 'overtake' and 'undertake' to be related opposites, yet their meanings are not connected.

He used to overtake too often and now he's with the undertaker.

15

Activity with text

Analyse the following using the categories above.

> 1 A cartoon shows a butcher standing in front of his shop, looking with a puzzled expression at the signs on the two shops on either side of him: Butch/Butcher/Butchest
> 2 A price list in a hairdresser's: Shampoo and set: £5; Genuine poo and set: £10.
> 3 I'm on a seafood diet. I see food and I eat it. (*badge*)
> 4 (*Speaking on telephone*) It's a polystyrene factory. (*Pause*) No, it makes polystyrene.
> 5 Does a nightnurse look after the night? (Roger McGough)

Commentary

The ambiguity in 1 is caused by the suffix '-er' which has two separate uses in English: to make a noun, often from a verb, meaning the person who does that, as in 'teacher'; or to form a comparative from an adjective, as in 'quick' – 'quicker'. In 2 the single morpheme word 'shampoo' (Hindi) has been treated as a compound word made up from 'sham' + 'poo'. In 3 there is also an ambiguity of sound, which allows the compound word 'seafood' to be treated as two separate words. The relationship of meaning between the two words in compounds is not fixed, which allows an ambiguity in 4: either a factory *made out of* polystyrene, or a factory *for making* polystyrene. There is a similar ambiguity in 5: a 'nightnurse' is a nurse who works *at night*, though a psychiatric nurse is one who *looks after* psychiatric patients.

Lexis

'Have you heard the one about the woodpecker?'
'It's boring.'

A common source of puns is the lexicon, or vocabulary, of English, which is vast and has borrowed from a variety of language sources: Celtic,

Germanic languages, Latin, French, Greek etc. **Homonyms** are pronounced the same and have the same spelling, but are two different words, which originate from different sources and so have a separate entry in the dictionary. A fishmonger who calls him/herself a 'Sole Trader' is referring to the two meanings for the word 'sole': one comes from the Latin 'solum' meaning 'bottom' or 'pavement', so is used to name the bottom of a shoe or a fish with a similar shape; the other comes from the Latin word 'solus' meaning 'alone'. This is slightly different from the fact that a single word like 'skip' can have various related meanings, referred to as **polysemy** (see below.) Often it is hard to know whether something is a homonym or a polyseme, without consulting a good etymological dictionary.

What makes a tree noisy? Its bark.

This example counts as a homonym, as the dictionary lists 'bark' under two separate entries: the sound of a dog from the Old English 'beorcan' and the other from Old Norse 'borkr', perhaps related to 'birch'.

As mentioned above, **polysemy** refers to the phenomenon of words having various, related meanings. Unintentional humour can occur in translations, as it is hard even for a good dictionary to explain all the subtle distinctions between the uses and senses of a word. For example, a notice in the toilet of an Italian train gave instructions for its use:

Deeply depress the stud.

English speakers rarely use the literal meaning of 'depress' = press down, so the metaphorical sense is the first to be understood, particularly as it occurs before 'stud', which can mean both a 'knob' or a 'young man noted for his sexual prowess'.

Prepositions in any language are polysemous, in that their use covers a wide range of meanings, which need to be defined in the context in which they occur. Prepositions often occur as part of fixed phrases, or idioms (see below), which cannot be understood by the meaning of the individual parts. In an episode of the sitcom *Friends* there was an exchange between Ross and Rachel, who had been on the brink of a relationship throughout the series. Rachel had left a message on Ross's answerphone, which he comments on in a literal way:

You said you were *over* me. When were you ever *under* me?

Phrasal verbs are sometimes referred to as 'multi-word' verbs. Some verbs in English are not single words but include a following preposition (or particle) as the unit of sense. The following contrasting pairs of sentences should help to make the distinction clear between a verb + a preposition and a phrasal verb. I *ran* up a hill./I *ran up* a bill. This becomes a source of ambiguity in jokes.

> When is a car not a car? When it *turns into* a garage. (When it *turns into* a garage.)

The meaning of phrasal verbs cannot be worked out from the meaning of their parts, i.e. the verb + preposition. To 'turn up' does not mean the opposite of to 'turn down'. Jokes like the following make this lack of logic apparent. (A phrasal verb may contain more than one preposition.)

> The trouble with Ian (Fleming) is that he *gets off with* women because he can't *get on with* them. (Rosamond Lehmann)

Idioms are groups of words that should be regarded as a single unit, as their meaning cannot be worked out from the constituent parts: 'go bananas'. There is ambiguity, if the group of words can be interpreted both as an idiom and as individual words:

> (miserable)   (resulted)
> When *down in the mouth*, remember Jonah. He *came out* all right.
> (in mouth of whale)   (out of mouth of whale)
>   (Thomas Edison)

Words can be grouped as belonging to a field of meaning ('firm, obstinate, stubborn'), but they have different **connotations**: 'I am firm, you are obstinate, s/he is a pig-headed fool.' The words 'skip, gambol, scamper, toddle' all describe a type of lighthearted, perhaps shaky movement, but their **collocations** are different: 'gambol' is a verb usually collocated with lambs. People can use the phrase 'I must be toddling off' but not 'I must be scampering off'. In the following witticism 'snow' is in a similar lexical field to 'slush', but the former has connotations of purity and the latter has connotations of unpleasantness and dirt:

> I'm as pure as the driven slush. (Tallulah Bankhead)

Activity with texts

Analyse the following using the categories above and mark where the ambiguity occurs. Use a good etymological dictionary to check whether words are homonyms or polysemes.

1　Contraceptives should be used on every conceivable occasion. (*The Last Goon Show of All*)

2　(*Pointing to the cemetery*) Did you know this is the dead centre of Sheffield? People are dying to get in there.

3　My problem lies in reconciling my gross habits with my net income. (Errol Flynn)

4　There are only two kinds of pedestrians – the quick and the dead. (Lord Thomas Robert Dewar)

5　Asked if she had nothing on in the calendar photo, she said: 'I had the radio on.' (Marilyn Monroe)

6　Some people are always late, like the late King George V. (Spike Milligan)

7　*Poem to my Goldfish*
Going round and round in a tank
with his mouth hanging open.
Bit like being in the army really.

8　(*Notice in a butcher's shop*) Would mothers please not sit their babies on the bacon slicer, as we are getting a little behind with our orders.

9　(*Cartoon showing a person sitting at a table in an exam, looking amazed as his pen escapes*) While answering a question on surrealism, his pen ran out.

10　Man in a bar: 'I just got a bottle of gin for my mother-in-law.' 'Sounds like a good swap.'

Commentary

The ambiguity lies in two possible interpretations of these words: 'conceivable', 'dead' and 'dying', 'gross', 'quick', 'late', 'tank', 'behind'. You will find that they are all polysemes, where the earlier meaning of the word has acquired a metaphorical sense, or, in the case of 'behind', a euphemistic sense. 5, 9 and 10 are ambiguous because of two possible interpretations of prepositions used in set phrases: 'have *x* on', 'run out', 'get *x* for'.

Syntax

Squad Helps Dog Bite Victim

Man Eating Piranha Mistakenly Sold as Pet Fish

Juvenile Court to Try Shooting Defendant

Ambiguities often occur in headlines because they are abbreviated and occur before the context. Although such puns are often deliberately used to catch attention, they are sometimes unintentional. These examples are not simply a case of individual words having double meanings, but the fact that there are two possible ways to group the words in relation to each other. The ambiguity is easily resolved by rephrasing. It's a dog-bite victim that the squad helped; a man-eating type of piranha was sold; a defendant in a shooting case is going to be tried.

Syntax refers to the way that meaning is created by the structure of words in a sentence. The way phrases are structured and the way clauses are structured are looked at in turn. If you are not familiar with the terms for analysis of phrase and clause structure – shown by letters above the words – concentrate on the rephrasing of the sentences, shown in round brackets.

The structure of phrases works in this way: each phrase must have a **headword** (h), with the option of **modifiers** (m) added before or after it.

        m   h   m
The damp *fog* [over the river]. (It's a damp, over-the-river sort of fog.)

The surface structure may look the same: there are headwords and modifiers, but there can be two interpretations of the deep structure, i.e. which modifier goes with which headword:

We will sell gasoline to anyone in a glass container.
(We will sell gasoline *in a glass container to anyone.*/We will sell gasoline *to anyone who is in a glass container.*)

Two possible interpretations of phrase structure can cause ambiguities in the way that headlines, notices etc. are read. These are examples of unintentional humour: 'For sale: Mixing bowl set designed to please a cook with round bottom for efficient beating.'

You can show, by phrase structure analysis and labelling, which headword you understand the modifier to be attached to. Or you can simply rephrase the sentence to show how the parts are related.

'Our son was involved in a terrible road accident.'
'Yes, the roads are terrible round here.'

(Hale and Pace)

     m   m   h
Intended sense: terrible road accident
(The accident was terrible. 'Terrible' modifies 'accident'.)

     m   h
Interpretation: [terrible road] accident
(The road was terrible. 'Terrible' modifies 'road'.)

To explain the ambiguity in some jokes requires a technical level of **clause** analysis, using terms to indicate the function and relationship of parts of the sentence: **subject, verb, object, indirect object, complement, adjunct** (or **adverbial**). However, everyone can perceive the two possible interpretations of sentence structure, even though they can't apply the labels - for example, the ambiguous headline in the next activity.

Read through the following brief explanation of clause analysis and then attempt the following activity: The structures of clauses (simple sentences) in English follow several main patterns using different elements. One essential element is the **verb** - which may be a single word or a group - and the **subject**, which normally comes before the verb. The simplest pattern is these two elements alone:

S   V
Time / flies.

Following the verb can be one, or more, of the remaining elements. If the verb is intransitive (does not require an object) there may be an **adjunct** (sometimes called adverbial). Adjuncts are single words or groups which add information about how, when or where the action happened. Here is an example:

S   V   A
Time / flies / like an arrow.

Graffiti added to this sentence revealed another interpretation of the structure:

S   V O   S   V   O
Fruit flies / like / a banana. Time flies / like / an arrow.

The verb is now understood as 'like', and 'a banana' or 'an arrow' is the **object**, i.e. *what* the flies like, rather than *how* they fly.

Another clause element is the **complement**, which has a different function from an object, as it adds more information about the subject, rather than introducing another person or thing as an object. Compare these two sentences to see the difference:

> S   V   O   S   V   C
> Jane / kicked / a doctor. Jane / became / a doctor.

The final clause element is the **indirect object**. Some verbs, like 'give' and 'send', can be followed by two objects: the direct object actually 'given' or 'sent' and the other the person to whom it was 'sent':

> S   V   Oi   Od
> He / found / her / a rose.

Compare the apparently similar sentence to see that the meaning of the verb 'found' changes and the final word now functions as a complement to the object:

> S   V   O   C
> She / found / him / a pig.

Some humour works by revealing ambiguities in the way the structure can be interpreted, for example: 'Call me a taxi.' 'You're a taxi.' The normal interpretation of the request - 'Call a taxi for me' - is as follows:

> V   Oi   Od
> Call / me / a taxi.

The odd interpretation of this structure as 'Address me as a taxi' has a different structure:

> V   O   C
> Call / me / a taxi.

Activity with text

Label this headline to show the two different interpretations of its structure.

> Police found drunk in shop window.
> Police found drunk in shop window.

Commentary

The ambiguity lies in whether 'drunk' is perceived as the object or complement.

    S   V   O   A
Police / found / drunk / in shop window.
(Police found a drunk person in the shop window.)

    S   V   C   A
Police / found / drunk / in shop window.
(Police were found in a drunk state in the shop window.)

There is a further ambiguity between the active verb 'found' and the passive verb '[were] found'.

Syntax and deixis

The next two jokes rely on the fact that 'serve' is a di-transitive verb, i.e. you serve *something to someone.* As you can omit either the direct or indirect object, this can cause ambiguity.

'We don't serve *coloured people.*'   (meant as indirect object)
'That's fine by me. I just want *some roast chicken.*'
    (understood as direct object)

'Do you serve *frogs' legs?*'   (meant as direct object)
'We serve *anyone who's able to pay.*'   (understood as indirect object)

23

Another cause of ambiguity in the English language is the fact that the **conjunction** 'that' can be omitted. This rarely leads to ambiguity, but it can be exploited for such in humour, as in 'We all know [that] disco rules'. A poster advertisement for insurance companies uses a picture of the musician Jools Holland, and creates an attention-catching ambiguity:

'Do you know two insurance companies have merged?'
'No, but you hum it and I'll play it.'

This is similar to the older joke: 'Can you sing *very softly, far away*', where the listener may understand part of the sentence structure as the title of a song and therefore the object, rather than as adverbs or the adjunct.

In all these examples, listed as syntax, the important thing is to be aware that there is no single word that has two meanings, but that it is the structure that can be interpreted in two different ways. There is one further type of ambiguity – of **pronoun reference** – which will be grouped under syntax. Notice, however, that these confusions are also caused by the joke-creator being deliberately awkward and refusing to pick the most likely sense of the comment. This lack of 'co-operation' in language use is discussed further in the next unit.

Deixis comes from a Greek word meaning 'finger'. It describes the function of certain words in a language to point, or refer, to something. Pronouns like 'it', 'he', 'she', 'they' are deictic terms, as you need the context in order to understand their reference. (They refer back or forwards: **anaphoric** and **cataphoric reference**, respectively.) This feature of language is used to create ambiguity, as in the joke question:

The Mississippi is the longest river in the USA. Can you spell it?
(I T spells 'it'.)

The questioner is deliberately misleading and alters the stress and intonation in order to suggest that 'it' refers to the word 'Mississippi'. Although there is great potential for ambiguity in language, the context normally makes it clear, so there would be no real confusion about the intended meaning of this teacher's comment:

All eyes on the blackboard and watch me run through it.

'It' refers not to the blackboard but to the exercise the teacher had presumably referred to earlier.

Activity with text

Analyse the following to show the two possible interpretations of the syntax. Group them under the headings of phrase structure, clause structure, deixis. Either use the labels for phrase and clause analysis or show the ambiguity by re-phrasing in two ways.

1   I have read your book and much like it. (Moses Hadas)
2   The students are revolting.
3   Dr Livingstone I Presume - the full name of Doctor Presume
4   Yoko Ono will talk about her husband John Lennon who was killed in an interview with Barbara Walters.
5   I once shot an elephant in my pyjamas. How he got into my pyjamas I'll never know. (Groucho Marx in *Animal Crackers*)
6   Make up for your life. (*advert*)
7   In passing sentence the judge said he was a thoroughly evil man. (*news report*)
8   'My parents are stuck at Waterloo Station. There's been a bomb scare.' 'Are they safe?' 'No, bombs are really dangerous.'

Commentary

Clause:

S V   O   +   A   V   O
I / have read / your book / and / much / like / it.

S V   O
I / have read / your book and much like it.

S   V   S   V   C
The students / are revolting. The students / are / revolting.

name   C   S V
Dr Livingstone I. Presume. Dr Livingstone / I / Presume.

Yoko Ono will *talk* about her husband John Lennon who was *killed* / in an interview with Barbara Walters / = adjunct to either 'talk' or 'killed'.

25

```
       V          O
   Make up for / your life.
```

'Make up for' = verb meaning 'compensate', or a noun phrase with the headword as 'make-up'.
Phrase:

I once shot an *elephant* [in my pyjamas].

The head word being modified is 'I' or 'elephant'
Deixis:

In passing sentence the judge said *he* was a thoroughly evil man.

Are *they* safe?

'He' could refer to the defendant or to the judge himself; 'they' could refer to bombs or to the parents.

Extension

The examples that you have looked at so far have been jokes constructed for a laugh. Humour is used as a device to attract attention for other purposes. It is used in advertising, for example, with the main purpose of persuading people to buy the product or use the service. It is used in headlines to create interest in reading on. The deliberate creation of structural ambiguity may be used in other types of text. Collect examples of texts that use structural ambiguities, and discuss the purpose of such humour.

You may have noticed that most of the jokes quoted in this unit relied on a question and answer format. Frank Muir ('Told in the Tuck-shop', *Times Literary Supplement*, 1978) calls this format 'riddles' and suggests that its continuing popularity is probably due to the fact that 'it gives the asker a tiny superiority. He knows something that the party of the second part does not know and has to admit that he does not know.' Compile the jokes and riddles that are current in your circle, assess whether most of them do follow this question and answer format, and discuss Muir's hypothesis concerning their popularity.

The shock of the new

This unit continues to examine humour which is caused by incongruity in language. Whereas Unit 2 looked at examples of *double* meaning in language, suggesting an image of language having a surface with something underneath, the work in this unit relies on the image of a *net* for the complex web of conventions that construct meaning. Some people even talk about language as a linguistic straitjacket. The German nonsense poet, Christian Morgenstern, used this sort of image to claim that we are imprisoned by language and that this causes our unsatis-factory relationship with other people, the society and the world in general. What we need to do, he said, is 'smash language' before we can learn to think properly. Some contemporary humour, like that of *Monty Python*, moves from wordplay towards nonsense and the absurd. But it is not a modern phenomenon. John O. Thompson points out that the French writer, Rabelais, used a comic form of speech called *coq-a-l'âne* (meaning 'from rooster to ass'): 'It is a genre of intentionally absurd verbal combinations, a form of completely liberated speech that ignores all norms, even those of elementary logic' (Thompson, 1982). But it is extreme to claim that such humour is '*completely* liberated' and 'ignores *all* norms'. If language is 'smashed', is there any firm basis from which it can be examined? It should be possible to discuss how the existing conventions of language have been *stretched* to reveal wider possibilities for language and thought.

Activity with text

The *Goon Show* written by Spike Milligan and Peter Sellers, has been described as 'the birth of alternative comedy' (Eddie Izzard). Look at this extract, where Eccles and Bluebottle are talking about the time. Jonathan Miller comments that Milligan's humour jokes about representation and logic — areas of interest to psychologists investigating the deep structure of thought. Notice how it plays with, and disturbs, our notions of 'time'. (No commentary follows.)

'What time is it Eccles?'

'Just a minute. I've got it written down here on a piece of paper. A nice man wrote the time down for me this morning.'

'Then why do you carry it around with you, Eccles?'

'Well, if anybody asks me the time, I can show it to them.'

'Wait a minute, Eccles my good man.'

'What is it, fellow?'

'It's written on this piece of paper that it's eight o'clock.'

'I know that. When I asked the fellow to write it down, it was eight o'clock.'

'Supposing, when somebody asks you the time, it ISN'T eight o'clock.'

'Then I don't show it to them.'

'So, how do you know when it's eight o'clock?'

'I've got it written down on a piece of paper.'

'I wish I could have a piece of paper with the time written down on it. Here, Eccles, let me hold that piece of paper to my ear, would you? (*Pause*) Here, this piece of paper ain't going!'

'What? I've been sold a forgery. No wonder it stopped at eight o'clock.'

Activity with text

Look at these examples. There are no double meanings, but do you think that they involve a type of incongruity? If there are elements of surprise, innovation and rule-breaking, there must be something else that you expected. As a language-user, you (and the teller) share a set of conventions, if not rules, about how language usually works.

(*Pilots in space ship*) It's no good, Dawson! We're being sucked in by the sun's gravitational field and there's nothing we can do! . . . And let me add those are my sunglasses you're wearing! (Gary Larson cartoon)

(*Two workmen eating sandwiches, balancing on a girder miles above the ground*) You ever get that urge, Frank? It begins with looking down from fifty storeys up, thinking about the meaninglessness of life, listening to dark voices deep inside you, and you think, 'Should I? . . . Should I? . . . Should I push someone off? (Gary Larson cartoon)

A man who was tried and acquitted for armed robbery said, 'Great. Does that mean I can keep the money?'

INFORMATION BOOTH
'Can I help you?' 'I'd like some information.' 'Yes?' 'What information have you got?' (*Fry and Laurie*)

This parrot is no more. It has ceased to be. It's expired and gone to meet its maker. This is a late parrot. It's a stiff. Bereft of life, it rests in peace. If you hadn't nailed it to the perch, it would be pushing up the daisies. It's rung down the curtain and joined the choir invisible. This is an ex-parrot. (*Monty Python*)

Two cows in a field. One says, 'Moo.' Other says, 'You bastard, I was going to say that.'

I was thrown out of college for cheating in the metaphysics exam; I looked into the soul of the boy next to me. (Woody Allen)

Commentary

These examples of humour are not so straightforward to explain, because they involve a wider set of conventions than those involving ambiguity of meaning. So, what are the usual conventions of language behaviour that are being broken? Here is a brief comment about each example.

There are accepted conventions about the type of things we would say if faced by imminent death – not a 'by the way' complaint about borrowed sunglasses. We recognise phrases like 'meaninglessness of life' as signals for confession about personal angst, not a homicidal urge. When someone tells us how much they are suffering, it is not enough to offer them a cookie. In a courtroom we would keep quiet about our guilt if we had pleaded 'not guilty'. We understand the sorts of questions that are suitable at an information booth. Clichés and other set expressions, like 'Do you believe everything *x* tells you?', are not to be taken at face value. Euphemisms are a way of skating delicately around the subject of death, not poured out in a torrent. We do not think of animals having a range of language choices, as humans do. Souls are not things to be looked into, and it's odd to think of it as a way of cheating.

Yet these examples of humour are not nonsense. They open up a range of possibilities — it's conceivable that animals do have just as sophisticated a system of communication; if you could look into another's soul, it might tell you much more than a book; why not expose the lack of sense in clichés, and who knows what might seem important at the point of death?

Semantics, pragmatics, discourse and register

The conventions of language in use are examined in the following sections on **semantics, pragmatics, discourse** and **register**. Each section outlines some concepts and terminology, with short examples of humour to illustrate them. The activities ask you to apply the concepts to humorous texts.

SEMANTICS

Semantics is the study of meaning. It examines relations of sense between words, for example **synonyms** (such as 'woman', 'lady', 'adult female being human'), and **antonyms** ('lady', 'gentleman'). However, not all aspects of meaning are describable without reference to a wider context. Semantics also takes into account the **connotations** of words, i.e. the communicative value they have apart from their reference. For some people 'lady' signifies more respect than 'woman', as it has connotations of gentility. Connotations can vary and change; today some people find the term 'woman' more acceptable. This is partly caused by the **collocations** of these terms, i.e. the way that they are used and the words that tend to occur with them. The collocations of the terms 'woman' and 'lady' are not the same: we say 'dinner-lady' not 'dinner-woman'. They do not have a similar range of collocations to 'man' and 'gentleman': in Wimbledon there is a 'Ladies' Final', but a 'Men's [not 'Gentlemen's'] Final'.

Sometimes we are caused to laugh by combinations of words and meanings that seem odd, or incongruous, in some way. Why is it that some combinations of words make sense together and others do not? Compare:

1 My uncle always sleeps in the day.
2 My uncle always sleeps awake.
3 My uncle always sleeps standing on one toe.

Because the second and third are also recognisably English, rather than gibberish, this sort of combination is being referred to as 'non-sense' rather than 'nonsense'. It is useful to think of two kinds of non-sense. The second example *contradicts what we know about language and meaning*, with the contradiction between 'sleep' and 'awake'. The third *contradicts what we know about the world* - it is not physically possible to sleep on one toe.

Apparent contradictions

The strange thing is that, rather than rejecting such odd examples of language, the human mind often reacts by trying to make sense of them, as in Chomsky's example: 'Colourless green ideas sleep furiously'. In creative uses of language, such as poetry, the new combinations are exciting precisely because they *extend* the range of possible meanings and cause a sudden shift in perception. The apparent contradiction 'bitter-sweet' invites a fresh look at the concepts of sweetness and bitterness; the meaning of the words is widened to include **metaphorical** senses. Perhaps the opposite is true of **clichés** - once a phrase is familiar, it is used without thought and bypasses the mind; certainly the metaphorical force loses its initial impact. For the sake of economy in language and to reduce human experience into orderly chunks, it is useful to have many such pre-packaged phrases. The poet is a person who 'unties the string'. The same may be true of the apparent contradictions of some humour, which force the mind into a 'cognitive shift'. Alexander Pope defined wit as 'what oft was thought, but ne'er so well expressed'. The stand-up comedian Eddie Izzard leaves his audience startled by observations which are strangely familiar (see Unit 8). In the following he points out a type of non-sense:

Prince Philip shoots things. He's the President of the World Wild Life Fund and he shoots things. 'Oh look, there's a panda. I'll protect them and then shoot them dead.'

There is an apparent contradiction in the meanings of 'protect' and 'shoot', and an actual contradiction in having a president of such an organisation who kills wildlife.

Three terms - contradiction, paradox and oxymoron - are used to describe this type of semantic incongruity. Their use overlaps, so it is difficult to distinguish between them. **Contradiction** is in everyday use for statements that are necessarily false. These can occur in slips of the tongue, which have been collected as unintentional humour in 'Colemanballs' (*Private Eye*):

We estimate, and this isn't an estimation, that Greta Waitz is 80 seconds behind. (David Coleman)

The term **paradox** is often used in logic for a self-contradictory proposal such as 'This statement is not true'. In literature the term **oxymoron** refers to statements which are seemingly absurd, even if actually well-founded, such as the example of 'bitter-sweet'. In order to make a satirical comment, the following are presented as oxymorons:

Tory Party

Socialist Worker

Military Intelligence

A **tautology**, however, is a statement which is true by virtue of its meaning alone, as there is apparently needless repetition. Slips of the tongue account for such utterances by sports commentators, collected and recycled in the columns of *Private Eye*:

Hurricane Higgins can either win or lose this final match tomorrow.
(Archie McPherson)

As this is communicatively empty, tautologies can also be termed nonsense. Sayings that occur in everyday speech are apparent tautologies, like 'What's done is done', but they do make an emphatic point, so are not devoid of sense. The sitcom *Brittas Empire* plays with semantic relations. The first example seems to state the obvious; the second has a type of twisted logic.

Criminals – they can't be trusted.

I brought a brick to break the window with. And a spare brick in case it's double glazing.

Activity with text

The novel *Catch-22* (Joseph Heller, 1961) has been so influential that its title is now part of the English language. It is listed in *The Concise Oxford Dictionary* as meaning 'a dilemma or circumstance from which there is no escape because of mutually conflicting or dependent conditions'. In the following extract the army doctor is explaining Catch-22 to the hero, Yossarian, who is so desperate to stop flying bombing missions that he decides that he will go crazy in order to be 'grounded'. Briefly explain the conditions of Catch-22, to show the contradictions that make it impossible for anyone to benefit from the rule.

'You're wasting your time,' Doc Daneeka was forced to tell him.

'Can't you ground someone who's crazy?'

'Oh, sure. I have to. There's a rule saying I have to ground anyone who's crazy.'

'Then why don't you ground me? I'm crazy. Ask Clevinger.'

'Clevinger? Where is Clevinger? You find Clevinger and I'll ask him.'

'Then ask any of the others. They'll tell you how crazy I am.'

'They're crazy.'

'Then why don't you ground them?'

'Why don't they ask me to ground them?'

''Because they're crazy, that's why.'

'Of course, they're crazy,' Doc Daneeka replied. 'I just told you they're crazy, didn't I? And you can't let crazy people decide whether you're crazy or not, can you?'

Yossarian looked at him soberly and tried another approach. 'Is Orr crazy?'

'He sure is,' Doc Daneeka said.

'Can you ground him?'

'I sure can. But first he has to ask me to. That's part of the rule.'

'Then why doesn't he ask you to?'

'Because he's crazy,' Doc Daneeka said. 'He has to be crazy to keep flying combat mssions after all the close calls he's had. Sure, I can ground Orr. But first he has to ask me to.'

'That's all he has to do to be grounded?'

'That's all. Let him ask me.'

'And then you can ground him?' Yossarian asked.

'No. Then I can't ground him.'

'You mean there's a catch?'

'Sure, there's a catch,' Doc Daneeka replied. 'Catch-22. Anyone who wants to get out of combat duty isn't really crazy.'

There was only one catch and that was Catch-22, which specified that a concern for one's own safety in the face of dangers that were real and immediate was the process of a rational mind. Orr was crazy and could be grounded. All he had to do was ask; and as soon as he did, he would no longer be crazy and would have to fly more missions. Orr would be crazy to fly more missions and sane if he didn't, but if he was sane he had to fly them. If he flew them he was crazy and didn't have to; but if he didn't want to he was sane and had to. Yossarian was moved very deeply by the absolute simplicity of this clause of Catch-22 and let out a respectful whistle.

Commentary

The paradox can be shown clearly if the logical connections in Catch-22 are spelt out:

1   can be grounded - *IF* crazy *AND* ask to be grounded
2   *IF* ask to be grounded = *not* crazy
3   *IF* fly missions   = crazy

The imposibility lies in the fact that there are two conditions that must both be met in order to be grounded (1). These two conditions are then said to be mutually exclusive, or contradictory (2): in other words it is logically impossible – by the terms of Catch-22 – to ever satisfy both conditions. The final paradox (3) is that the authorities agree that it is crazy to fly missions, but not crazy to want to stop. As with all humour, the timing plays an important part. Although the paradox can be stated very briefly, the dialogue moves step by step, so that the reader's apprehension of the absurdity of Catch-22 is drawn out as slowly as the protagonist's. The element of disguise is also important to humour. The final paragraph, where Yossarian spells out the paradox, acts like a punchline, where some of the pleasure often occurs because the audience is marginally ahead of the teller.

Metaphor and simile

Another type of semantic incongruity occurs in **metaphor** or **simile**. It may seem strange to class these as apparent contradictions. They do, however, present quite different images. 'O, my Luve's like a red red rose' (Robert Burns) is a good example of a simile. These figures of speech are an admired feature in literature. What makes their effect humorous? It may be that the image is bizarre or awkwardly incongruous:

> Football is a cruel mistress, she's more than a mistress, she's a wife, she's a mother, she's a daughter, she's an errant child. (Peter Cook as Alan Latchley)

A cause of unintentional humour is the use of **mixed metaphors**, usually two clichéd expressions joined together without awareness of the strange images created. This is seized on and repeated as soon as a politician, or any public figure, does this.

> A lot of people think the hard noses of Fleet Street don't have a soft centre, but they do you know. (Gerald Williams)

This clumsy use of language can then be used in scripted humour.

The term **conceit** is used for an extended metaphor, found, for example, in metaphysical poetry: John Donne compares himself and his mistress to the two points of a compass, seeming to travel far apart, but always connected. Something similar happens in humour where an original or strange **analogy** is made. In the radio programme *The Hitchhiker's Guide to the Galaxy* the basis of the situation is: 'Let's imagine that people are hitchhiking round the galaxy . . .'.

Similar to this extended analogy is the use of an incongruity between language and situation for a shorter piece of humour. Many of the cartoons by Gary Larson superimpose the language and habits identifiable with one group (usually familiar modern humans) onto a quite different group. In this example there is a picture of galley slaves. One has his hand up and is complaining to the overseer.

> Mr Mathews! Mr Mathews! I just went to the restroom and Hodges here took my place. It's my turn for the window seat, Mr Mathews.

Another conceptual shift comes when Gary Larson portrays the animal world in human terms (or is it the other way round?). He shows one female praying mantis calling on another.

> I don't know what you're insinuating, Jane, but I haven't seen your Harold all day – besides, surely you know I would only devour my OWN husband.

It is interesting that this type of humour is not usually found on television, where the bizarre situation would have to be created with costume and special effects. (*Red Dwarf* keeps to a fairly basic set.) It is found in cartoon form, or on the radio, where the listener can visualise any strange scene suggested. A Radio 4 game involved placing characters from one fictional text into another and devising the new scene. Examples of incongruous mixes were: Billy Bunter in the last scene of *Hamlet*; and the heroin addict, Sick Boy, from the film *Trainspotting* being introduced to Elizabeth Bennet by Darcy in *Pride and Prejudice*. Creating impossible situations can be done in stand-up comedy, where a single person speaking can create flights of fantasy in the mind. One of Eddie Izzard's triumphs was a piece about a bird on a jumbo jet, gradually getting used to the strange sensation of being a flying creature flying, then playing with all the gadgets, while his jealous mate was peering in through the porthole.

Some contemporary humour pushes the boundaries of language beyond a strange but conceivable idea, as in the next example from Vic Reeves and Bob Mortimer introducing a *Blue Peter* type of activity:

> And a boy from Eton will be ripping the guts out of a monkey and showing us how to make a saxophone.

to the line which caps it, which is hard to find sense in at all:

> Yes, Bob, and I'm going to be making a cello out of Andre Agassi.

Children also appreciate this form of **surreal** humour. In the series of 'elephant jokes', there is sense in the punchline only if you assume that elephants both paint their toenails and hide in jam:

> When do elephants paint their toenails red? When they want to hide upside-down in strawberry jam.

It has been suggested (Wales 1989) that children can cope with these surreal images because they are familiar with the world of fairy tales and cartoons, where such personification is common. Absurd and surreal elements have a much wider appeal than that, certainly since the *Goon Show*, but it is not a twentieth-century phenomenon.

So far this unit has examined ways in which humour makes unusual semantic connections in apparent tautology or contradictions. As well as using language creatively, humour can also refer to the nature of language, especially any pre-packaged phrases – idioms or clichés: 'They're head over heels in love.' As someone commented – *all of us* do *almost everything* head over heels. If we are trying to create an image of people doing cartwheels etc., why don't we say they're 'heels over head' in love? This sort of self-reference to language itself draws attention to the wording of sayings so familiar that they are used without thought of the meaning:

'Pheebs, you wanna help?'
'Oh, I wish I could, but I really don't want to.' (*Friends*)

Reference to language itself is also a factor when humorists slightly alter the wording of well-known sayings:

Save a little money each month and at the end of the year you'll be surprised at how *little* you have. (Ernest Haskins)

The term **intertextuality** is used when you need to understand that a reference is being made to an existing text. Some humour refers to existing styles and conventions of humour itself. You have to understand how 'elephant jokes' usually work to appreciate that the common sense answer is surprising:

What would you do if an elephant sat in front of you at the cinema? Miss most of the film.

Activity with text

Performance poetry has moved into venues like pubs, and attracts a younger audience than traditional poetry readings. 'Slam poetry' has the audience participating by judging the poets, so the poems' appeal has to be immediate and contemporary. Comment on the type of humour and the way in which it is created in these two poems by Neil Gauckwin (*Some You Win, Some You Slam*, Guffaw Productions, 1997) and one by Sophie Hannah (*Hotels Like Houses*, Carcanet Press, 1996):

Handbag
We wanted a lizard skin handbag
instead of the real thing.
It seemed less cruel.
Who wants a bag made out of hands anyway?
Only enough room for two scrunched up tissues
and a few other things.

Interior Design
Throwing a brightly coloured piece of material
Over a sofa
Makes it look more interesting.

Pity the same can't be said for some people.

Slow It Right Down
Nobody gets priority with you
So all concerned must do the best they can:
Be safe and stop, be brave and charge on through -
You are an unmarked crossroads of a man.

Some men I know are double yellow lines
Or traffic lights for everyone to see.
I'm practised when it comes to give way signs
But unmarked crossroads are a mystery

And this time I shall do it by the book,
Slow it right down and read my highway code;
Before reversing, take one final look -
An unmarked crossroads down an unknown road.

Commentary

The image suggested of a lizard-skin handbag is deliberately misleading. It takes a moment for the reworking of the word 'handbag' — bag made out of hands — to sink in. The poem ends quickly, leaving a bizarre image and a fresh look at the notion of cruelty. Most of the audience would react unfavourably to animal skin used for bags — how much worse is it to use human skin? The second poem also begins with an accepted notion — an almost clichéd style of decor — and simply extends the logic from furniture to people. Sophie Hannah uses an unusual metaphor for love, and extends the image throughout the poem. There is something incongruous about such a prosaic image of road features. As the device itself alludes to the conceits of metaphysical poetry, there is an element of humour in such modern images. Most people can find a revealing comment on the necessary dangers of love in 'Be safe and stop, be brave and charge on through'.

PRAGMATICS

The term **pragmatics** is used to refer to the ways that sentences acquire meanings in contexts. Sometimes factual knowledge and assumptions are required to understand the significance. It is not enough to understand the meaning of the word 'box' and that Pandora is a girl's name; you have to be familiar with the myth about Pandora opening a box freeing ill-omens, to understand this cartoon by Gary Larson:

> (*Cartoon of teacher facing class with gift box on table*) And the note says, 'Dear classmates and Ms Kilgore: Now that my family have moved away, I feel bad that I whined so much about being mistreated. Hope the contents of this box will set things right. Love, Pandora.' ... How sweet.

There is also an important distinction between the **sense** and **force** of an utterance. 'You make great coffee', taken in isolation, can be seen as imparting some information. This is its 'sense'. In context it can be used to convey a variety of messages – its 'force' is different in each case.

1   Do I make good coffee?   You make great coffee.
2   Do you think I'm a good cook?   You make great coffee.
3   It's your turn to make the coffee. You make great coffee.

The philosopher of language J. L. Austin moved away from asking 'what do sentences mean?' to 'what sort of act do we perform in uttering a sentence?' This area is referred to as **speech act theory**. There are possibilities for ambiguity of meaning when there is a gap between the sense and force of the utterance. Misunderstandings happen when a person concentrates on the structural *form* of the utterance, rather than being aware that it can have various *functions*. Billy Connolly points out the strange way that parents frame their complaints, refusals and threats:

That's right, leave your clothes all over the floor.

I'll give you bike.

I'll make you smile on the other side of your face.

Another possible cause of ambiguity lies in the indirect way that English speakers frame utterances to make them more polite: 'I wonder if you would shut the door?' 'Do you? Let me know if you work it out.' The question might be: How do people know which interpretation to make of an utterance? The philosopher H. P. Grice suggests ways of explaining the relation between sense and force in his **cooperative principle** of conversation: that is to say we assume that people in conversation are co-operative and follow these maxims:

> *Quantity*
>   Give the right amount of information.
>   Make it as informative as possible.
>   Do not give more information than required.
> *Quality*
>   Try to make it true.
>   Do not say what you believe to be false.
>   Do not say something for which you do not have enough evidence.
> *Relation*
>   Be relevant.
> *Manner*
>   Be clear.
>   Avoid obscurity of expression.
>   Avoid ambiguity.
>   Be brief.
>   Be orderly.

In the following example the first speaker does not give enough information by using the term 'woman' (maxim of quantity) and so allows an ambiguity, i.e. could be 'another woman' (maxim of manner) (Clark and Clark in Leech 1974: 122):

A: I saw Mr X having dinner with a woman yesterday.
B: Really? Does his wife know about it?
A: Of course she does. She was the woman he was having dinner with.

B has made a reasonable assumption that the woman was not his wife. Grice calls this **conversational implicature**. Sometimes it is not the speaker who breaks the maxims of conversation but the listener. In the next case B makes an unreasonable assumption about the reference of the deictic term 'my'.

A: I didn't sleep with my wife before we were married, did you?
B: I don't know. What was her maiden name?

Activity with text

Comment on the ways that the co-operative principle is being broken in the following. (No commentary follows this activity.)

'Have a nice day!' 'Thank you, but I have other plans.'

Does your dog bite?' 'No.' (*Bends down to stroke dog and gets bitten*) 'I thought you said your dog didn't bite?' 'It's not my dog.' (Billy Connolly)

'Did you imagine you'd live here for twenty years?' 'No, I didn't imagine it – I really did.' (*People Like You*, Radio 4)

Stewardess: There's a problem in the cabin?
Passenger: What is it?
Stewardess: It's a little room at the front of the plane where the captain sits, but don't worry about that now. (film *Airplane*)

'We have the largest country in the world [USA]. They used to tell us at school that some of our states are as big as France and England put together.' 'Ah, you must find it very draughty, I should fancy.' (Oscar Wilde)

DISCOURSE

The term **discourse** is used to describe the rules and conventions underlying the use of language in extended stretches of written and spoken text. Efficient listening and reading involve prediction from clues and signals: the audience is usually one jump ahead. The openings of texts often create certain expectations about what will follow. These expectations are then subverted in humour:

England's not a bad country - it's just a mean, cold, ugly, divided, tired, clapped-out, post-imperial, post-industrial, slag-heap covered in polystyrene hamburger cartons.

(Margaret Drabble)

Discourse also refers to the conventions of conversation and dialogue: knowing the appropriate range of responses at stages in the conversation:

'Sorry to trouble you.'
'Not at all.'
'Thank you very much. Good day.'
(Morecambe and Wise)

Users of the language understand conventions for the overall structure of types of discourse. There is the expectation in 'Englishman, Scotsman, Irishman' jokes, for example, that the first two set up a pattern and the punchline comes with a twist on the third. In a more general way, there is an expectation that three parallel pieces of language build up to a climax; in humour there is often an anti-climax. In the US sitcom *Cheers* the bartender, Woody, asks whether he should ask for a rise in pay. His colleague says 'You're a good bartender, you're never off sick, you don't have holidays. I wouldn't bother.' Humorists often create bitingly witty comments by using the technique of this three-part structure (see next section on register) yet insert surprisingly incongruous terms:

I require only three things of a man - he should be handsome, ruthless and stupid. (Dorothy Parker)

Children begin by loving their parents. After a time they judge them. Rarely, if ever, do they forgive them. (Oscar Wilde)

We met Dr Hall in such very deep mourning that either his mother, his wife, or himself must be dead. (Jane Austen)

Activity with text

Comment on the way this breaks the usual expectations of stories – that the questions raised will be answered. (No commentary follows this activity.)

A rabbit goes into a butcher's shop and asks, 'Have you got any lettuce?' The butcher says, 'We don't sell lettuce here. You need the greengrocer's across the road.' The next day the rabbit comes into the shop and asks for some lettuce again. The butcher tells him, 'Look, I told you yesterday, we don't sell lettuce. You need the greengrocer.' The rabbit comes in the next day and asks the butcher again, 'Have you got any lettuce?' The butcher goes mad. He says, 'Look, I'm sick of this. How many times do I have to tell you I don't sell lettuce. If you come in here again asking for lettuce, I'm going to nail your ears to the floor.' The next day the rabbit comes in and asks the butcher, 'Have you got any nails?' 'Nails? No.' 'Right,' the rabbit says, 'Have you got any lettuce?'

REGISTER

In linguistics the term **register** is used in a way analogous to a musical register, which can range from high to low tones. There is the notion of a 'high' or formal register in language and a range including more casual registers. The scale from formal to informal is an oversimplified view of the range of styles that even individual language-users can employ, as they shift their style of language to make it appropriate to the situation. The 'situation' encompasses whether you are speaking or writing; what your purpose is; whom you are addressing, even your topic. People make fine adjustments over the day: talking to a friend, talking to a stranger, talking on the telephone, writing a message on the blackboard. Some styles are more definitely set and these are recognised as genres, like headline-style, where the language is abbreviated; the style of estate agents' brochures; pulp sci-fi style.

The Top Tips page in *Viz* imitates a recognisable style:

Housewives – why waste time and energy mashing potatoes? Simply place a large spud under each of hubby's car tyres last thing at night. When he drives off to work in the morning, hey presto, instant mash.

The markers of this style are the direct address in the opening question, the use of cheery terms like 'hubby', 'simply' and 'hey presto'. Even the lexis falls within the expected field: 'mashing potatoes', but the notion itself is odd.

Some **rhetorical devices** are so familiar that they signal a grand speech-making style. One is the pattern of building up balanced phrases in threes – but in humour, the final one drops in register, for a sort of anti-climax. Another is the use of a balanced structure, often with a lexical contrast. The patterning helps to emphasise the point being made.

> Anything that is too stupid to be spoken is sung. (Voltaire)

> 'The soul is born old but grows young. That is the comedy of life.'
> 'And the body is born young and grows old. That is life's tragedy.'
> (Oscar Wilde)

When using language in a variety of everyday contexts, people shift from one register to another. Joos (1961) describes styles of speaking and writing on a five-point scale of degrees of formality:

intimate – use of a 'private' code, rather than 'public' vocabulary, e.g. jargon
casual – between friends, so using shortened forms and slang
consultative – coming to terms with strangers, supply background information
formal – no participation from audience, can stand alone: detachment, cohesion
frozen – ritualised forms, e.g. in ceremonies and legal language.

To be socially competent you have to have access to all of them and select the one appropriate for the situation. A lot of humour uses register to reveal some problem a person is having with a situation, because they select the wrong register or clumsily mix registers.

Sometimes there is the attitude that the features of written language are intrinsically superior and that any sort of abbreviation is sloppy. This causes people to 'talk like a book' when they feel out of their depth. 'Malapropism' (see p. 11) refers to the mis-use of familiar expressions, which suggests an attempt to use a higher register than the speaker is comfortable with. Most people would admit that mistakes occur when experimenting with language and using expressions for the first time. This sort of unintentional humour is as likely to happen with highly educated people (as you saw in a previous example), but it tends to be used as a stereotyped language feature of less educated characters in scripted humour, as in the following extract from the radio series *The Glums.*

MR GLUM: Cor lummy, Ted – you ask more questions than the *Spanish Imposition*. As *perchance* would have had it, that whole get-up of Ron's did not cost us a penny.
LANDLORD: You got that entire outfit for free?
MR GLUM: Absolutely *au gratin*. ('The Job Interview')

As Joos (1961) says, people can switch between styles, but we do not normally expect a jump of more than one move. **Bathos** is a sudden switch in style, from one which has grand overtones to one which is commonplace:

> She can make you laugh, she can make you cry, she can bring tears to me eyes, she can bring blood to me shoulders, she can bring the kettle to the boil. (Peter Cook as Alan Latchley)

There is a shift in the other direction in the following:

> Why did Napoleon behave in the way he did? First of all, by all accounts, he was a bit of a short-arse and you know what they say about small men. They only come up to your Adam's apple and don't like it so they have to compensate by becoming Emperor of France. (Jo Brand)

Anachronism is a type of incongruous mixture of reference to things which never existed at the same time:

> Jesus was also well-known for his miracles, and probably would have formed a band if Smokey Robinson hadn't done it. (Jo Brand)

Activity with text

Comment on the uses of register to create humour in the following examples.

(*A series of five frames depicting Tarzan practising his chat-up line*)
Okay ... 'How do you do. My name is Tarzan and I believe you are known as Jane.'
'Allow me to introduce myself ... I am Tarzan, Lord of the Jungle ... And you?'
'You must be Jane. I am Tarzan. It's a pleasure to meet you.'
(*There she is.*) 'Me Tarzan. You Jane.'
(Damn.)

(Gary Larson)

(The Far Side by Gary Larson © Farworks, Inc. Used with permission. All rights reserved)

(*Lawyer proposing to a woman.*) I love you, Sharon, and these documents will advise you of certain rights you have under federal and state law.

(*A cartoon offers this version of a politician's resignation speech.*) I decisioned the necessifaction of the resignatory action/option due to the dangerosity of the trendflowing of foreign policy away from our originatious careful coursing towards consensitivity, purposity, steadfastnitude, and above all, clarity.

(Jeff MacNelly)

Right, I'm your official guide. Now before I show you round, I'll just fill you in on a few details, as we call them. As you can see, we're standing in the hall of the Haworth Parsonage, where Hawarth's parson, the Reverend Brontë, lived here with his daughters, the famous Brontë sisters, now alas, no longer with us – but they have left their novels – which I've not read, being more of a Dick Francis nut. Now, if you pass by me into the parlour (mind my vaccination) ... This is what was known in those days as a parlour, somewhat similar to our lounge-type sitting room in modern terminology. I'm afraid the wallpaper isn't the original period to which we're referring to; it's actually Laura Ashley, but I think it does give some idea of what life must have been like in a blustery old Yorkshire community of long ago.

(Victoria Wood, *Brontëburgers*)

Commentary

It is recognised as a lack to have access only to casual registers. Tarzan is rehearsing more formal ways of greeting someone and introducing oneself. In the heat of the moment, all he's left with is the casual.

It's not often recognised as a lack to only have access to the formal

– thought of as *the* good language. But the joke about a lawyer, stuck in a frozen register, shows that it is just as inept. Some people are protectively aware of their own 'superior' status and try to maintain a rigidly formal register of language, as well as dress and manners, in any situation. The effect may often be to impress their audience into nervous silence or agreement. The humorist, like the child in 'The Emperor's New Clothes', sees such language as covering up their nakedness of ideas, sense, sincerity etc. and reveals this by exaggerating the tendency to 'gobbledygook' – pompous or pretentious jargon. Jeff McNally follows the familiar morphological rules for word formation, but the politician's tendency is to prefer the long and complicated, even where a perfectly good version exists. The suffixes -*al* and -*atious* are both possible for adjectives; -*ity* and -*itude* are both used for abstract nouns, for example. This means that 'original' becomes 'originatious'; 'consensus – consensitivity'; 'steadfastness – steadfastnitude'. Rather than a 'punchline' the text leads up to a 'punchword'; after all the gobbledygook the final word 'clarity' is the only clear word used!

It can seem like a social gaffe to use an casual register in a formal situation. (It can, of course, be done deliberately to make a point about the speaker's attitude to the situation.) In scripted humour the device of mixing an informal language style with a formal situation creates incongruity. In the tour guide's speech there are colloquial lexical items – 'nut', 'lounge-type', 'blustery' – which would be more appropriate for informal talk between friends. There is also the strangely unneccesary explanation of the term 'details' and the personal reference to her 'vaccination'. The extract not only uses an incongruously informal register in parts but switches awkwardly between a formal, lecture-giving style – 'This is what was known in those days as . . . in modern terminology' – and a casual, conversational style. The phrase 'now, alas, no longer with us' comes from a frozen register, that of a rather high-flown funeral oration. When she uses a more formal register she gets the sentence structure confused: '*where* the Reverend Brontë, lived *here*'; '*to* which we're referring *to*'.

Allusion, context and parody

What makes something funny in one context and *not* funny in another?

Up to this point you have examined the ways in which humour is created by incongruity in language. This explains why something has the *potential* to be funny, but there remains a discussion of a wider context for humour – why does something make some people react with a laugh, but others with a groan or silence? Compare the following

47

examples of humour, both relying on similar structural features:

> What's the difference between the Prince of Wales and a tennis ball?
> One is heir to the throne and the other is thrown into the air.

> Mortimer: Do you remember that time I had a bad back?
> Reeves: You were like a Tina Turner concert after that.
> Mortimer: No, Vic – a concertina.

The types of wordplay in the first example are predominantly found in jokes for children, so they are not likely to appeal to a more sophisticated audience – the incongruity has been perceived, but is not as amusing. The second example occurred in a Vic Reeves and Bob Mortimer sketch. In this context the audience perceives both the wordplay and the **allusion** to this format as outdated. The corniness of such jokes is emphasised because the wordplay is clumsy and laboured, yet, perversely, this is what makes the audience laugh. You have to perceive the joke in these ways: understand the wordplay; consider such wordplay unfunny; and appreciate its occurrence in a new context. The following discussion of parody will show how the notion of **intertextuality** – or reference to existing styles – can help to account for differences in the reception of humour. (The term **postmodern** is used in various art forms, including literature and humour, where there is an interaction between historical memory and the new.)

The dictionary definition of **parody** emphasises the fact that it is a 'humorous imitation' of a style. In the rock musical *Forbidden Planet* much of the humour comes from a recognition of the way it refers to both the genre of sci-fi and Shakespeare's play *The Tempest.* In the new work of parody there is reference to an older, existing form, in that recognisable features of it are imitated; some of the most quoted Shakespearean lines are used with slight changes:

> 'Once more unto the *bridge* my friends.' (into the breech)

> '*Two bleeps* or not *two bleeps,* that is the question.' (to be)

In this sense parody is a parasitical form, which cannot exist without its 'host', but this need not mean that it cannot be original or creative. This consciousness of form is sometimes termed **self-reflexive** – the text encourages the reader or listener to focus on the style itself and be aware of a conflict or dialogue between the old style and the parodic version. There is a critical distance; the audience cannot be swept along by enjoyment of the text itself. The film *Wayne's World* has three endings, each using 'set-pieces' of a genre. For an audience unfamiliar with the cartoon series *Scooby Doo*, the literal unmasking of the villain in one ending would have no intertextual impact.

This may explain the very different reception of humour with elements of parody. It cannot be appreciated without reference to the context – the term **transcontextualise** means bridging two contexts. For example the television shows of Vic Reeves and Bob Mortimer can seem strange and annoying to an audience who are unaware of the existing showbiz conventions being distorted. Other contemporary television comedies rely on knowledge of specific allusions. One of the sketches in *Harry Enfield and Chums* (the title itself being an allusion) features a character called 'Mr Dead' who is propped up in a stable. Taken on its own, this seems pointlessly bizarre; the humour relies on knowledge of the old children's television show featuring a talking horse called 'Mr Ed'. A significant factor in some modern comedy is the reference to genres that were never considered great or influential; part of the impact is the very fact that they were considered 'naff' at the time. There are a number of ways that this can be signalled – to tell a joke and immediately add: 'B-boom' in the manner of Basil Brush, is one way. Perhaps this is similar to moves in fashion, where the notion of **retro** – imitation of a style from the past – often reinstates the most 'unfashionable' designs, but an older person wearing crimplene would not have the same effect. The element of self-awareness is essential, wearing the clothes 'in quotation marks'. Parody uses signals, which can only be recognised by an audience familiar with the original.

Activity

Videotape a television show, or collect written data, that has elements of parody (the magazine *Viz* for example). Identify the genres and styles that are referred to. Find examples of imitation of those styles and the ways in which these have been exaggerated or distorted. Try to assess the way it is received by different audiences. (There may be differences between age groups, for example.) When you have read the following section, comment on the purpose of such parody.

The purpose and effect of parody

This still leaves the question of the *purpose* of the parody, which can range from a playful imitation to harsh satire. Sometimes successful works inspire parodies, so there is an element of celebration of that style. This may well be the case in the references to Shakespeare in *Forbidden Planet*. The impressionist Rory Bremner imitates the voice and style of celebrities so accurately that he sounds just like the television sports commentator Desmond Lynam, for example. Yet there seemed to be no further cutting edge of satire: in fact, Desmond Lynam became more of a cult fugure after this, so the effect was not to make him ridiculous.

Sometimes, however, the style being parodied is a pretentious one that is being deflated by mockery: the style is challenged, in order to renovate and renew it. Where humour has a critical force, the term **satire** is used. (Unit 6 looks at examples of satire in literature.) As the novelist Nabokov says: 'satire is a lesson, parody is a game.' Other writers (such as Bakhtin and Kristeva) argue that parody can never have the force of satire, which seeks to undermine established attitudes, because - as the saying goes - 'imitation is the sincerest form of flattery'. Carnival, for example, was originally a form of parody of the existing social order, but it can be seen as an 'authorised transgression of norms'. Because it exists within that social order and is permitted - though strictly limited to a few days in the year - carnival may help to preserve the existing conventions.

In a similar way television parodies are also 'consecrated by tradition', in the sense that they are commissioned and produced by the same organisation as the form being mocked. Mrs Merton's parody of chat shows on Channel 4 may discredit the existing format - or, by imitation, may serve to enhance it. *Shooting Stars* was a parody of television game show formats, but there was no sense that the original game shows became less popular. Some original television shows like *Gladiators* and *Blind Date* (ITV) have such a rigidly set format, and catchphrases delivered with a knowing self-reference, that they could be seen as parodies of themselves. The presenters, contestants and audience are all laughing - a sort of 'conservative mockery', which forestalls any further parody, perhaps.

Although it is possible to identify a range of purposes for humour, it may not be clear what the writer's intention was, and there is no guarantee that the audience will receive it that way. So a further issue to discuss is the *effect* of humour. The form of **irony** is particularly vulnerable to misunderstanding, as it is: 'an expression of meaning, often humorous or sarcastic, by the use of *language of a different or opposite tendency*'. Examples from literature give clear examples of this. In *A Modest Proposal* by Jonathan Swift, his proposition that the famine in Ireland could be solved by eating babies was taken by some readers at its face value. Understanding the force of irony involves awareness of the language used and knowledge about the world. Attention is brought to the form because there is something incongruous about its use in that context. The mismatch between the language use and intended meaning is often subtle, which means that irony may not be perceived as such. The novels of Jane Austen use irony, both in the narrators' comments and in the words spoken by characters. *Pride and Prejudice* opens with this statement:

> It is a truth universally acknowledged that a single man in possession of a good fortune must be in want of a wife.

On the face of it, the sentence has an authoritative ring about it. Why don't readers take it at its face value? It sounds grand and philosophical because of its formal register - complex sentence structure and abstract terms, for example - but it is full of logical holes. This is partly because of the overstatement: 'universally', 'must be' and the apparent paradox between 'a good fortune' and 'in want of'. To perceive this contradiction, the reader also needs non-linguistic knowledge about the society.

This discussion of parody, satire and irony concludes the units dealing with the incongruity theory of humour. The following two units examine other aspects which influence the audience's response: the target and the topic of humour.

'My mother-in-law . . .'

The superiority theory

The philosopher Thomas Hobbes (author of *Leviathan*, 1651) characterised laughter as a 'sudden glory' at a triumph of our own or at an indignity suffered by someone else. This could explain why people laugh at the many variations of the slipping-on-a-banana-skin scenario; there's an urge to laugh at the (literal) downfall of another. Hobbes claimed that those who laugh are momentarily released from awareness of their own lack of ability. This accords with a commonsense perception of much humour being a form of mockery - a way of attacking others, so maintaining power and status by gaining support from others who join in the laughter. People most likely to laugh, according to Hobbes, are those 'that are conscious of the fewest abilities in themselves; who are forced to keep themselves in their own favour, by observing the imperfections of other men.' Ambrose Bierce offers this definition in *The Devil's Dictionary* (1957): 'CONSOLATION, n. The knowledge that a better man is more unfortunate than yourself.'

However, it would be hard to claim that this is the only cause of laughter, and many feel that it is the least desirable. Some instances of humour that attacks a target can be seen as cruel mockery of an already oppressed group by the insecure, but there is a long history of satire where the follies of those in power are exposed. There is also humour which makes a wry comment about the teller or human weaknesses in general. 'The aim of a joke is not to degrade the human being but to remind him that he is already degraded.' (George Orwell).

This unit examines the range of targets for humour, the stance - or intention - of the joke-teller and how this affects its reception by the audience or tellee. To count as humour, rather than simply an insult, there will also be some type of incongruity in the language used.

Activity with text

There *is* mockery in this sketch by Dawn French and Jennifer Saunders, 'Record Choice'. (A successful woman doctor is being interviewed on a show like *Desert Island Discs*.) What is the target of this humour and how do you respond to it? (No commentary follows.)

> Jennifer: Before we go for your Record Choice, let's see if we can paint a picture of the young Eleanor Wood, and maybe recall a few childhood memories for you. You excelled in school academically and at sport. I love to imagine this picture of you, this Cornish dumpling, probably goalie in the hockey team, cheerfully bouncing around in goal, lifting everyone's spirits. You were, I should imagine, a happy, jolly, sturdy person.
> Dawn: I suppose so.
> Jennifer: The class clown, perhaps? So many people with physical disadvantages like yourself often end up compensating. Was it, dare I say, your chunkiness, the fact that you were and are a fuller-figured person, that made you more determined to succeed? . . .
> Dawn: Oh all right, you can describe me as chunky, ample, bubbly, huggable and so on, as long as I can describe you as slow-witted, uninteresting, obtuse, dull, tedious, mentally stagnant . . . Because what you're really wanting to say about me is 'fat' and what I'm skirting around about you is 'stupid'.

LESS POWERFUL GROUPS AS THE BUTT OF HUMOUR

The term **butt** comes from Old French, originally referring to a mound behind a target. It is now used in a metaphorical sense meaning an object of ridicule and is used in phrases such as 'the butt of his jokes'. The interest for students of language lies in investigating *which* groups are the butt of humour, thus revealing something about the attitudes of that society.

> I wouldn't say she was pretty and I wouldn't say she was ugly – just pretty ugly.

There have been so many jokes about mothers-in-law in recent British humour that they are referred to as a type: 'mother-in-law jokes'; similarly with 'Irish' jokes. Some people claim that language simply *reflects* existing attitudes, that sexism and racism exist 'in the world' and that words do not change anything. Others maintain that language is a powerful weapon, and that making conscious decisions about the use of language can help to *form or change* attitudes. This latter position leads to a deliberate rejection of humour that relies on a portrayal of mothers-in-law as nagging and the Irish as thick, on the grounds that it tends to perpetuate harmful social divisions. The former position would regard this as a form of censorship which is, at best, pointless and, at worst, a dangerous form of thought control.

This division of attitudes towards language can be seen in arguments about 'political correctness'. This term has acquired unfavourable connotations, so it is better, perhaps, to use more neutral terms, like 'social awareness', to refer to the position that language has powerful implications. It is certainly true that there is a decline in the occurrence of 'mother-in-law' and 'Irish' jokes – in some circles, at least – but it is difficult to know whether this is because attitudes have changed, or whether attitudes changed because there was explicit control over language and joking.

In many examples of humour the butt is a representative of a group perceived as inferior in some sense, so it might seem unnecessary to create a sense of superiority over them. The butt must first be accorded some power. Certain social groups can be perceived as a threat, if not in any physical or economic sense, then because they shake the other's sense of security in themselves. These types of humour will, therefore, be context-bound: perceptions of status vary from culture to culture at any one moment and change over time. This partly accounts for varying responses to humour. Modern audiences feel uncomfortable with the bringing low of the characters of Kate in Shakespeare's *The Taming of the Shrew* and Shylock in *The Merchant of Venice*, for example, if forthright women and successful Jews are not felt to be a threat.

Extension

Collect examples where the butt of humour is perceived as inferior in some sense. See if some groups commonly recur. Do you agree that this gives a snapshot of the attitudes of the society at that time?

WHICH SOCIAL GROUPS ARE THE BUTT OF HUMOUR?

Representatives of lower social class groups are often the focus of humour. They are also identified with a region of the country.

What do you say to a Liverpudlian in a suit? 'When's the court date?'

In the film *Brief Encounter* the hero and heroine are securely middle-class and the plot deals with their tragic romance; the light relief comes in the characters of the railway porter and the woman serving tea, and they are each given a marked regional dialect. The comic interludes in Shakespeare's plays revolve around characters whose language use is clearly differentiated from those in the main romantic or tragic plot. There is a tendency to find some accents of English intrinsically funny – a 'Brummie' accent, for example. In Germany, the 'Plattdeutsch' (flat German) accent, spoken by people in the north, has a similarly low status. Exactly which group is considered to be ridiculous varies from culture to culture. In Britain jokes with the Irish as a butt used to be extremely popular: 'There was an Englishman, a Scotsman and an Irishman ...'. In Germany there are jokes with a similar structure. The butts of humour in these cases are always perceived to have some language deficiency.

The group is further stereotyped with one single characteristic: the Welsh and their affinity with sheep, the Scots with meanness, Essex girls with stupidity. This trait can then become more specific: the wearing of white high heels, dancing round handbags and the names Sharon and Tracey are used to signify 'thick' or 'common'. It is enough to listen to someone called Tracey explain how this makes her feel about her identity, to sense that language can be a powerful manipulator of attitudes.

In the previous extension activity you may have found jokes about gays, blacks, ugly women, women in general, all fat people, people with disabilities. There are many examples to support the theory that the *butts* of humour are often social groups who have less power and prestige.

Does this mean that those who laugh at the jokes agree that they are inferior or a threat? The stance of the **tellee** influences the response to this type of humour. Many people feel that racist jokes, for example, are offensive and do not laugh. But defence can come from surprising quarters. Roy Chubby Brown is known for his 'unremitting filth' and is censored to the extent that his act is never broadcast on television:

> Somebody told me not to go and see *Schindler's List* without a box of tissues. *Schindler's List*? I couldn't find anything to wank over in *Schindler's List.*

Although it is not a joke about the Holocaust, many people would find it offensive to combine a reference to the Final Solution with a gag about masturbation. Yet Harold Jacobson says: 'I, a Jew, feel more threatened by those who would wipe out ethnic jokes than by those who unthinkingly make them.' Certainly comedians like Bernard Manning claim not to be racist. Jacobson also suggests that the humour and laughter at a Manning performance is a self-reflective laughter about racism and sexism itself. This brings in an evaluation of the intention of the joke **teller**. An apparently sexist joke like 'Why do women have small feet? So they can get closer to the sink.', can sometimes be told with an element of mocking allusion to that very genre. However this does not guarantee that the tellee perceives the joke in the way it was intended. Johnny Speight discovered that his own ironic portrayal of Alf Garnett in *Til Death Us Do Part* was also enjoyed by people who held the racist attitudes expressed by the character; in other words the irony was not perceived.

Activity with text

Identify the butts in the following two extracts. How is the humour constructed? Is it possible to comment on the stance, or intention, of the teller? How do you – the tellee – respond to each? Compare your reactions with others in your group.

(*Two young females are talking at a bus stop*)
'So he walked over, right big I am, and he had tattoos up his arms right, an anchor here and a microwave here.'
'He didn't.'
'He did. He said do you want a drink or do you want a kick up the bum with an open-toed sandal. I said get you Eamonn Andrews.'
'You didn't.'
'I did. I said I'll have a pint of Babycham, some pork scratchings and a yellow cherry and if I'm not here when you get back I'll be in t'toilet putting hide and heal on my love bites.'
'You didn't.'
'I did.' ...
'So he puts down his banana fritter, he says Kelly-Marie Tunstall, just because I have tattoos and a hairy navel button does not mean I do not have the instincts of an English gentleman. Please believe me when I say I will be happy to escort you to your abode of residence, asking nothing in return but the chance of seeing you again.'
'He didn't.'
'No, he didn't. He caught the bus and I had to pay for my own lychees.'

Anne: Gosh, isn't it sad to think there are people in this world who are starving?
Dick: Yes - I suppose it is.
George: Still - if they didn't breed like rabbits there'd be more to go round.
Anne: Yes, that's true.
Julian: Mind you, half of them die in childbirth, so it must all even up in the end, I suppose.
Anne: Oh dear ... I do wish there was something we could do to help.
Dick: Poor old Anne - just like Anne to get het up about world problems on a lovely day like this.

Commentary

The butt in the first extract, from a Victoria Wood television sketch, is a working-class northern female, laughed at for being so 'common'. The caricature is created by the choice of name: 'Kelly-Marie Tunstall', and the reference to 'tattoos', 'a pint of Babycham, some pork scratchings', 'love bites'. There is a parody of register in the conversational refrain: 'You didn't.' 'I did.' – which leads up to the reversal in the last lines — and the use of present tense for relating a past event: 'So he puts down.' Whether this is seen as cruel mockery depends partly on the stance of Victoria Wood. Is she laughing at the butt for being working-class and northern? She has a sharp ear for the speech patterns of many social groups – particularly northerners like herself – and also deflates the pretensions of middle-class speech in her sketches. It is easier to determine the response of the tellee, i.e. whether your group found this funny without any reservations.

The device of irony is used in the second extract, from the Comic Strip film *Five Go Mad on Mescalin,* where the butts – representing racist attitudes – represent these views in an apparently self-congratulatory way.

POWERFUL GROUPS AS THE BUTT OF HUMOUR

As this last example shows, the butt of humour is not always in an inferior position. Much humour is an attack on people in superior positions of power and influence; in a sense, it is the fight-back of the victim, who has only words to use against money, might and status. Political satire is an example of this in the public domain - on radio, television and in the newspapers. People who don't have access to the media collect and spread jokes by word of mouth. There is a consensus among the joke-tellers that they have suffered, in some way, at the hands of these people: social workers, lawyers, celebrities like Paul Daniels. It doesn't seem to matter how corny the jokes are, they are exchanged and capped with yet another. Established joke formulas are used, like 'How many *x* does it take to change a light bulb?' and the punchline is altered appropriately.

Activity with text

Here are two examples of lawyer jokes. Collect other jokes that are currently circulating with a powerful, but unpopular, butt. Do they use established formulas? (No commentary follows.)

Why are laboratory rats being replaced by lawyers? For two reasons: the scientists get attached to the rats; and there are some things a rat just won't do.

What is the difference between a catfish and a lawyer? One is a scum-sucking bottom dweller, and the other is a fish.

Self-deprecating humour

In the following examples the humour involves the lower status of the teller, in relation to the butt. Some humour involves a complete reversal, where the usual butt of jokes - woman, working class, black etc. - turns the tables. The victim bites back in these cases:

> A definition of a Southern Moderate is a cat who'll lynch you from a low tree. (Dick Gregory)

Look, for example, at the following two jokes, which are similar in many respects. If you respond differently to them, it may be due to the reversal of the butt.

> A man and a woman are sitting at home in front of the fire. The man gets up and says, 'I'm off down the pub. Get your coat on.' 'Oh,' says the woman surprised, 'are you taking me out for a drink?' 'No. I need to put the fire out.'

> An elderly man and woman are sitting at home in front of the fire. The man turns to his wife and says, 'You know, I think I'd like to be cremated.' 'OK,' she says, 'get your coat on.'

Sometimes the tellers make themselves the butt of the humour. The female stand-up comic Jo Brand puts herself down for being fat, unattractive and desperate for a man: 'I'm not an opera singer - I just look like one.' There is a sort of power to get in first.

Self-deprecating humour need not always be so specific; some humorous writers target the foibles and weaknesses that they see as common to all human beings. Ambrose Bierce is often described as a cynic, as many of his definitions in *The Devil's Dictionary* (1957) have this characteristic.

> BORE, n. A person who talks when you wish him to listen.

Activity with text

Identify the butts of humour in the following and comment on the stance of the teller.

1   'How should they answer?' In reply to the question 'Why do Jews always answer a question with a question?' (Abigail Van Buren)

2   I never believed in Santa Claus because I knew no white dude would come into my neighbourhood after dark. (Dick Gregory)

3   Why are all single women thin and all married women fat? Because single women come home, take one look in the fridge and go to bed. And married women come home, take one look in the bed and go to the fridge.

4   You never see a Jewish mugger. They would never say, 'Give me your money or I'll kill you.' They say, 'Listen, you don't have to give me ALL your money. We'll have a cup of tea and a cake and talk about it.' They're not CALLED muggers; they are called lawyers and solicitors. (Jackie Mason, former rabbi)

5   I want to be the white man's brother, not his brother-in-law. (Martin Luther King)

6   Civil war in Yugoslavia? That's not going to get the washing up done or the beds made. (Jo Brand)

7   My girlfriend has left me. If that isn't bad enough, it was for someone who looks exactly like me. (Phil Nee, Chinese American comedian)

8   Woman: Do you think it's all right to wear erotic underwear, or do you think it's just pandering to patriarchal fantasies to the point where we've internalised male values so profoundly that we even take a narcissistic pleasure in the objectification of our own bodies?
    Friend: You're in a funny mood. (Jackie Fleming cartoon)

Commentary

There is an allusion to stereotypes of women in general, feminists and various ethnic groups in these examples, yet it forms a humorous critical comment on the accepted stereotypes, given the teller's membership of those groups. Examples 3 and 5 add an attack on the oppressing group. Example 4 has some classic features of humour, creating an incongruously soft version of mugging and leading up to the punchline which equates a lawyer's activities with robbery.

Extension

It has been said that language is like a badge. Much language serves as a way of establishing bonds with others, of working out who is with you and who is outside the group. Something similar is true of humour as well. Lundberg noted that, in a workplace, joking 'defines and re-defines the differentiated social groupings, reinforces the ranking of group members both within and between groups, and clarifies the status of one group to another' (Lundberg 1969 in Purdie 1993: 129). The impact of some humour comes from the fact that it is an 'in-joke'. This shows that it is just as important to understand the social relationships between the status of the teller, the tellee and the butt of the humour, as it is to understand other language devices used to construct the humour.

Collect examples of humour with a butt. Comment on the stance of the teller and the tellee to the butt. What is the purpose or effect of the humour?

Unit five

'Crikey, that's a hard one!'

Psychic release

The previous unit looked at examples of humour with a target. In the sense that it is used as a form of attack, the humour is part of a battle between groups in society. But some say that humour expresses some sort of battle within ourselves. According to Howard Jacobson (*Seriously Funny*, Channel 4) the historical Italian drama form *Commedia del'Arte* 'jeers at *all* our feelings and thus releases us from the torment of being ourselves'. Although he talked about sex and death, much of the series was concerned with the connection between comedy and human excreta! It seems convincing in some cases: the comedian Jack Dee said 'I still think there's nothing funnier than farts.' The psychic release theory of humour explains the triggering of laughter by the sense of release from a threat being overcome - such as a reduction of fears about death and sex.

This unit looks at the areas which *are* taboos (set apart as sacred or prohibited) but which *may* be mentioned - it is interesting, then, to see which areas stay strictly out of bounds. Like other ways of formulating taboos, joking helps to establish the bounds of what it is right to think and say, by breaking some rules, but keeping some limits. What are the taboos in this society, and are they same for all people? Have they changed in modern times? As with the superiority theory, the response varies according to the attitudes of the tellee - for example, older people tend to find obscenities more shocking, but age is only one factor. Other features make humour either acceptable or offensive: whether the language is explicit or uses innuendo; whether the presentation is fictional and general, or factual and specific. The first activity asks you to begin by considering your own response.

Activity with text

Do these cause laughter, offence or irritation for you? Is it possible to explain what makes you laugh? Who might find them funniest or most offensive?

1   If you're on acid and you think you can fly - take off from the fuckin' ground.
2   Gwendolyn, a young Welsh woman, returned from her honeymoon. Her mother asked how it went. 'Oh, mother, what a penis!' 'No, Gwendolyn, you mean "What happiness".'
3   Doctor: You've got acute angina.
    Female patient: I haven't got a bad pair of tits either.
4   (*Card showing a fox hunt in the background and a pair of hedgehogs watching in the foreground*) Caption: The hedgehogs weren't the only ones around with pricks on their backs that morning.
5   My brain is my second favourite organ. (Woody Allen)
6   Marriage is like a bank account. You put it in, you take it out, you lose interest.
7   When I'm good, I'm very very good, but when I'm bad, I'm better. (Mae West)
8   I had a cold shower and felt rosy all over. Then she slapped my face.
9   Three nuns who died were tested by St Peter before being allowed into heaven. He asked them a question in turn. 'What is the name of the first man?' 'Adam.' 'OK, go in.' 'What is the name of the first woman?' 'Eve.' 'Right.' Then he asked the third, 'What were the first words that Eve said to Adam?' 'Crikey, that's a hard one!' 'That's right. In you go.'

Commentary

The most common taboo area for humour is sex, as you can see from the limited range of topics in these jokes. One-off jokes about death and religion were harder to find.

Perhaps other subjects have replaced them in today's society: drug-taking has contemporary shock value. Sometimes the taboo word itself triggers a laugh — it is direct and the response is immediate. In these examples only the first one — not about sex — used the word 'fuck'. Such direct taboo-breaking rarely gets into print or the media. There has to be some sort of *disguise*, at least in the public domain. The reference to 'penis' and 'tits' was caused by one character misunderstanding. Other jokes alluded to a taboo word by the use of ambiguity: 'happiness', 'angina', 'pricks', 'organ', sometimes at the level of grammatical structure: 'I felt rosy.' There is a delayed response with innuendo: 'That's a hard one'. This sort of coyness often makes it acceptable. It's OK to hint, but offensive to say it out loud. This, in itself, says something interesting about our conventions of language use.

Extension

The previous examples represent humour found by the author of this book, in the 1990s. Collect examples of taboo-breaking humour current in your social group, to see if there is a different spread of topics and ways of creating laughter.

TABOOS: SEX AND EXCRETA

It is almost certain that the most common topics are still sex and excreta. This taboo seems to be universal. Children's jokes break the taboo of referring to bodily functions, but with an element of disguise. This tendency does not disappear with age.

What's the difference between a bad marksman and a constipated owl? One shoots but can't hit.

'We have to be able to mop, you see, with Dad's habits . . .'
'Dicky bladder?'
'We call him Dad . . .' (Victoria Wood)

Nor is it a recent phenomenon. Carnival was traditionally a time of cross-dressing, outrageous behaviour and freedom from the usual, social contraints – though only for a day or two. Sex has been a cause of laughter for as long as written evidence exists: 'If only it was as easy to banish hunger by rubbing the belly as it is to masturbate' (Diogenes the Cynic). In Chaucer's fourteenth-century 'Miller's Tale' the young lovers play a trick on Absolon, when he begs Alison for a kiss.

> This Absolon gan wipe his mouth ful drie.
> Derk was the night as pich, or as the cole,
> And at the window out she putte hir hole,
> And Absolon, him fil no bet ne wers,
> But with his mouth he kiste hir naked ers
> Ful savourly, er he were war of this.
> Abak he stirte, and thoughte it was amis,
> For wel he wiste a womman hath no berd.
> (*The Canterbury Tales*)

In *Seriously Funny* (Jacobson 1997) Howard Jacobson emphasises the origins of laughter in the ancient roots of civilisation, when we were closer to our animal nature. He claims that we laugh at slapstick comedy because the buckets of water and custard pies remind us of urine and faeces. Mikhail Bakhtin, the Russian literary critic, traced this tradition from the Greek satyr plays which originated in the phallic songs and dances for the worship of Dionysus. Even at the height of Athenian civilisation the performance of a great tragedy, like *Oedipus*, alway ended with a rude comedy involving satyrs – the mythical creatures, half-human, half-animal, notorious for their genital endowment and insatiable sexual appetite. (In the twentieth century, Barry Humphries' character, Les Patterson, is a leering, satyr figure.) This form of humour does not have to exclude women: in Aristophanes' play *Lysistrata* the women mock men's enslavement to their phalluses. Female comedians today can be just as explicit in their sexual references.

All this suggests that sex, though a taboo, does not fall outside the boundaries of socially acceptable humour. Yet limits are imposed. In the USA, in the 1980s, the Comedy of Hate pushed the boundaries so far that it could be broadcast only in a severely censored form, even on late-night documentaries. However 'free' people consider themselves, they still draw a line at some point and say: 'That is not funny, but offensive.' It is not so much the topic itself as the treatment of it.

One factor which influences the audience response is the use of euphemisms or **innuendos**, rather than explicit language or taboo words:

> The decorating-mad couple always fell off the bed when *making love*, because they wanted a mat(t) finish.

66

Once a particular object has sexual connotations, that word can be enough to trigger the laugh: 'bananas', 'cucumbers'. A word or phrase may have a double meaning. Some words, like 'balls', are polysemes, and the homophone 'pear/pair' creates a number of corny gags *à la* Benny Hill: 'What a lovely pear.' The teller can then blame the tellee for 'having a dirty mind'.

Billy Connolly comments on the use of the archetypal taboo word: it is 'strong' language, in the sense that it has a powerful effect.

> People say it's a limited vocabulary that makes you swear. Well, I know...127 words, and my favourite is still 'Fuck'. There is no English equivalent for 'fuck' – 'Go away' 'Shoo'? You couldn't say: 'Fuck off,' he hinted.

The force of taboo words changes from one social group to another. Restrictions have loosened about what words can be printed and broadcast, but they still increase the tendency to laugh. Compare your reaction to the joke from Unit 2: 'When is a car not a car? When it turns into a garage', and this similarly constructed ambiguity, which adds shock value – and topical reference.

> Why are monkeys like acid rain? They both fuck up trees.

Activity with text

Read the following examples. Is sex the only taboo to be broken? Would it be more acceptable if innuendo was used, rather than explicit taboo language? (No commentary follows.)

> This is the idea that has made me virtually an anonymous figure in America for the last ten years.... If you have children here tonight, I'm sorry to tell you this, they are not special. Don't misunderstand me, I know you think they're special, I'm aware of that. I'm just telling you they're not. Do you know that everytime a guy comes he comes two hundred million sperm? And you mean to tell me you think your child is special?? Do you know what that means? I have wiped entire civilisations off my chest – with a grey gym sock! *That* is special.
>
> (Bill Hicks)

> Princess Diana is always complaining. 'I'm not happy. I'm not happy.'
> She married one of the richest men in the world. His mother owns
> England, Ireland, Scotland, Canada, New Zealand, Australia. By sleeping
> with Prince Charles, one day she will own - listen to the verb, own -
> England, Ireland, Scotland, Canada, New Zealand and Australia ...
> Then I say, 'I would screw a duck for Rhode Island. What does she want?'
>
> (Joan Rivers)
>
> * The context for this piece has changed. The target of the humour was Princess
> Diana and the comments were made while she was alive. Since her death, the com-
> ments cross over the line between what is felt to be acceptable and what is not.

TABOOS: DEATH

Death is another taboo. This does not mean that it can not be mentioned
at all but that there are restrictions - one is the use of respectful or
euphemistic terms. Humour on the topic of death also ranges from the
generally acceptable to the shocking and offensive. The following
witticisms are based on the ability to find humour in references to our
own mortality and involve an allusion to a well-known saying, which is
turned around in some way.

Eat, drink and be merry, for tomorrow we may diet.

The trouble with life in the fast lane is that you get to the other end
in an awful hurry.

Although joking about death *in general* can occur on television - 'Since I
have been manager of this leisure centre, there have only been twenty-
three deaths and not one of them a member of staff (*Brittas Empire*) - once
the reference is to a *specific* death it is classed as a 'sick' joke and occurs
only in the private domain. As soon as a terrible disaster happens, it is
only a matter of days before jokes spread around the country by word of
mouth, in the way that urban myths do. After the Challenger space
shuttle disaster the following riddle appeared:

What does NASA stand for? Need another seven astronauts.

Even in this area, some taboos exert a stronger influence - there have
been no jokes (as far as this writer has noticed) about the shooting of a

class of primary school children in Dunblane, for example. Some tragedies seem to be acknowledged as too important for humour, but there is still variation in the response. Gerry Sadowitz was playing in Sheffield on the night of the Hillsborough disaster, where ninety-seven football fans died, and he included references about people getting crushed to death. Many people booed and walked out, but quite a few laughed. Does this mean that they lacked the finer human sensitivity of the the protesters? Sadowitz himself claims that there are no limits - anything goes. This point will be discussed in later activities.

Activity with text

What taboo-breaking occurs in this sketch 'Fat Aristocrats' by French and Saunders? What factors make it acceptable, so that it stays within the limits of broadcast humour?

(*Pouring whisky from her binocular case into two old teacups*)
A: There we go. Picked it up at the wedding.
B: What a bloody dull do. Bride looked a fright, I thought.
A: What a fright! Like some old bitch on heat, I thought. Pig in a dress. She may be my daughter but I'll have to agree with you there!
B: Thank God we had a reason to get away.

A: Bloody lucky, I mean lot of fuss and nonsense there was when George passed away. Do you remember?
B: What?
A: The other week when George passed away.
B: George?
A: Husband. You know George. Stupid looking bugger. Gammy leg.
B: Oh yes. George.
A: Very sick at the end, poor George. Very sick.
B: Bad luck.
A: Stripped of his faculties. Took me aside, asked me if I'd help speed up the going ... put him out of his misery with a bit of dignity.
B: And did you, dear?
A: Had to. Hit him over the head with a shovel and dumped him on the bonfire.
B: Well, it's what he would have wanted. Marvellous compost.
(*Feast of French and Saunders*, Heinemann, 1991)

Commentary

Although taboos are being broken – calling her daughter 'some old bitch on heat' and her husband 'stupid-looking bugger' – the participants are fictional; there is no actual death. The audience is laughing at, not sharing, the crude attitudes of the old women. The sketch is clearly marked as humorous. There is parody of an upper-class register with the clipped sentences: '[He was] Stripped of his faculties' and phrases like 'lot of fuss and nonsense'. There is incongruity in the sudden shift of register from euphemisms like 'speed up the going . . . put him out of his misery with a bit of dignity' to the plain 'Hit him over the head with a shovel and dumped him on the bonfire'. Any taboo words used have become acceptable: 'bloody dull'.

TABOOS: RELIGION

Religion is the third taboo area to be examined. There is still a blasphemy law in Britain - it can be a crime to make offensive references to the Christian religion. In practice the decline in church attendance seems to go along with a decline in the amount of shock caused by flippant, or offensive, references to religion. Although the *Monty Python* film *Life of Brian*, about a Messiah figure called Brian, caused outrage in some circles, it was popular and has been shown on mainstream television.

Extension

As you have already seen with the other taboo areas discussed, the *way* that the topic is treated can push it across the boundary of acceptability. Compare the following extract from the stand-up comedy of John Dowie (Rosengard and Wilmut, 1989) with the extract from the previous activity. You should see that it has a number of factors that would make it too offensive to be broadcast.

The Vatican said two things not long ago, guaranteed to make everyone's life so much better and happier ... the Vatican said, 'It's still a sin to be a homosexual and it's still a sin to wank.' Well, the Vatican didn't say 'wank' obviously. The reason why the Pope doesn't like homosexuals and masturbators is because they don't breed, hardly at all. The Pope likes people to be Catholics and breed. And make more Catholics - and they breed - and make more Catholics and more Catholics ... all those Catholics go to church and give all their money to the Pope. And he spends all their money on a long white dress with an artificial hand, and underneath - he's wanking all the time ... I'd like to go back two thousand years, stand at the foot of the crucifix and say to Jesus Christ, 'Do you know what you're doing *means*?' 'Yes, I know what it means, actually, thank you very much ... I don't get nailed to a piece of wood for no fucking reason. Of course I know what it means. I'm taking the sins of the world on my shoulders - through me you shall be redeemed.' 'It's got fuck all to do with that, pal ... two thousand years from now - no wanking.' 'What? No wanking? Are you mad? You think I got nailed to a piece of wood to stop people wanking? It stops *me* wanking, I agree.' 'And no homosexuals.' 'What? Do me a favour! Haven't you noticed I hang around with twelve men all the time? It was snogging with Judas that got me into this mess in the first place. Who's been filling your head full of all this crap?' 'The Pope.' 'Who's he?' 'He's in charge.' 'I'm in fucking charge, pal - I'm in charge - I'm the Bruce Forsyth of this particular gig.' ... Interesting, also, isn't it? - the Pope drives around in a car with bullet-proof glass in the windows ... and Jesus Christ never wore nail-proof gloves, did he?

Commentary

First there is the use of taboo words that are still 'out of bounds'. The reference to religion is not general, but specific. Another taboo is broken when explicit references to sexuality are linked to revered figureheads of the Christian religion. And there are flippant comments about the death of Jesus: for anyone who holds this as sacred, this degree of incongruity is offensive, not funny. Indeed, the purpose of the piece is not light-hearted humour but an angry criticism. Formal limits that are set on humour mean that such a piece is restricted to the relatively private domain of an adult comedy club. (See Unit 8 for further discussion on the limits on live comedy.)

The context for taboo-breaking humour

You have seen that various factors influence the response to humour: the topic; whether the language is explicit or uses innuendo; whether it is framed as fictional or real; the use of humorous devices, like incongruity. What other factors can influence the audience to laugh or not?

There are limits on the time and the place for humour. It is conventional to find jokes in certain contexts: some joke formulas have become running gags, like '*x* do it *y*' which are popular on bumper stickers. Other formulas are found on notices in workplaces and on greetings cards. It is interesting that such double entendres are rarely found on Christmas cards and *never* on Easter cards, or cards commemorating the birth of a baby or expressing sympathy for death. Certain taboos remain in force, yet occasionally humour pushes against these boundaries.

People usually signal first that they are going to tell a joke, so that the listeners are ready and willing to laugh. Sometimes this established context - of joking - can override the actual content, so that people laugh without taking time to decide whether they find it funny. This may seem an extreme example of co-operation in conversation. But the context can often determine whether something is received as humorous. Roger McGough is known as a performer of humorous poetry. He was doing a show in a theatre in Sheffield, each poem funnier and more absurd than the last. As the laughter subsided from one, he announced the next: 'This one's about a young woman who got raped by a jogger.' Laughter broke out in sections of the audience. 'Is there something funny about that?' There was a ripple of uncertain laughter - was his deadpan expression part of the joke? He was so offended by the laughter that he was no longer the comedy poet but a headteacher, lecturing a hall of kids on their appalling behaviour. The audience sat silently through his serious poem, but were too nervous to laugh much when he reverted to his usual comic style.

Activity

Debates about censorship usually hinge on drawing the line between what is and is not acceptable for a given society. Those who push the boundaries in one direction usually set firm limits in another area: Jim Davidson − known for his 'blue' jokes − finds the *Spitting Image* caricatures of the Royal Family offensive.

Are there limits on humour for you? Or do you feel, as Gerry

Sadowitz says, that 'anything goes'? Find an example of humour with elements of taboo-breaking that are potentially offensive. Explain your response to it.

This unit concludes the examination of theories of humour. The final three units each look at a genre of humour and apply this framework of analysis to them.

Written texts – literature

The term 'literature' covers such a wide spectrum of genres and styles that it is not possible to do more than indicate approaches to humour in this area. It is useful to think of three main divisions: drama, prose and poetry. Under each heading some issues are discussed to guide your own selection of texts for analysis. The text provides one example of the way that the framework suggested in this book can be applied to literature. The activity section then hands over to you to select genres and texts for further investigation.

Drama

In drama the term **comedy** is often used to characterise a particular sort of play, as distinct from **tragedy**. In broad terms a comedy ends in marriage, a tragedy ends in death. The notion of human relationships and sex as the necessary ingredient of comedy may not seem as obvious as death being a necessary part of tragedy - there are more romantic views perhaps! The comedies of Shakespeare certainly end in multiple marriages, the plot involving confusion and setbacks to the - usually - young lovers. The obstacles are often put in their way by the older generation, or the prevailing social conditions that dictate who is a suitable mate. This overall structure also characterises the comedy dramas of Oscar Wilde. Plays termed 'farces' involve little more than sexual romps, with less subtlety of characterisation or plot.

Leaving aside such broad comments on the structure of a comedy, close language analysis will need to focus on particular instances of humour within the drama. Humorous interludes in the tragedies and historical plays of Shakespeare introduce characters designated as comic, for example the fool in *King Lear*. The comic characters are often drawn from working classes - Shakespeare uses a range of regional dialects, though this may be less noticeable to a modern audience. These humorous interludes are also signalled by a change in style - prose for the comic characters, poetry for the tragic - and noble! - characters. This tendency to stereotype social classes as inherently either 'comic' or 'tragic' still happens in today's dramas - more so in films than in stage plays perhaps.

The humour in Shakespeare plays tends to rely on wordplay, often with a sexual innuendo. In *Romeo and Juliet*, Mercutio teases Juliet's Nurse with a play on the words 'hare' and 'hoar', meaning grey with age, but sounding like 'whore'.

> No hare sir, unless a hare sir in a lenten pie, that is something stale and hoar ere it be spent. (Act 2 scene 4)

He can make a pun, even when dying:

> Ask for me tomorrow, and you shall find me a *grave* man. (Act 3 scene 1)

Activity with text

Apart from double meanings, there are other ways of creating verbal humour. The comic plays of Oscar Wilde may be termed 'comedy of manners' as they deal with the romantic intrigues of a leisured, moneyed class. The overall stance is a wittily cynical view of society's accepted attitudes.

Comment on the ways in which humour is constructed in these examples from the play *The Importance of Being Earnest*, by Oscar Wilde. His plays are noted for their wit, but this is not based in double meanings. You should find below examples of the types of humour discussed in Unit 3.

1   The amount of women in London who flirt with their own husbands is perfectly scandalous. It looks so bad. It is simply washing one's clean linen in public.

2   You don't seem to realise, that in married life, three is company and two is none.

3   I do not approve of anything that tampers with natural ignorance. Ignorance is like a delicate exotic fruit: touch it and the bloom is gone.

4   If one plays good music people don't listen, and if one plays bad music people don't talk.

5   (*Describing a novel*) The good ended happily, and the bad unhappily. That is what Fiction means.

6   To be born, or at any rate bred, in a handbag, whether it had handles or not, seems to me to display a contempt for the ordinary decencies of family life that reminds one of the worst excesses of the French Revolution.

7   In matters of grave importance, style, not sincerity, is the vital thing.

8   The two weak points of our age are its want of principle and its want of profile.

9   Relations are simply a tedious pack of people, who haven't got the remotest knowledge of how to live, nor the smallest instinct about when to die.

10 It is always painful to part from people whom one has known for a very brief space of time. The absence of old friends one can endure with equanimity. But even a momentary separation from anyone to whom one has just been introduced is almost unbearable.

Commentary

The values of the Victorian world, and perhaps of the twentieth century, are mocked in witty one-liners. The style Oscar Wilde adopts has a familiar, authoritative ring to it, so that the twist in meaning takes a moment to sink in. These often begin with definite statements: 'I do not approve of anything'; 'It is always painful'. Then they drop into a well-known saying, or a neatly balanced structure. By slightly shifting the wording, he jolts our expectations. He takes a cliché (1, 2) and changes 'dirty' to 'clean'; 'three' to 'two' and vice versa, so that the resulting saying is a reversal of the accepted view of marriage. The simile of a 'delicate exotic fruit' (3) challenges the accepted view of ignorance as an undesirable state. The others use a balance of structure with related semantic items: 'The good ended happily, and the bad unhappily'. This suggests a neat and watertight case, until you notice the unexpected twist – cynically suggesting that in real life the good end unhappily. Once the notion of 'grave importance' is mentioned, 'style' seems incongruous; as does the linking of 'principle' with 'profile'. Example 6 uses a different rhetorical style, which builds up in a long sentence, with many digressions: 'or at any rate', 'whether or not', 'seems to me' This all suggests that the speaker is taking the time to be absolutely precise. The final comparison that is offered is a ridiculous overstatement, 'the worst excesses of the French Revolution', that undermines the impression of authority and good sense.

Extension

Collect examples of films and plays marketed as comedies, and consider whether these three features occur: a plot structure that deals with obstacles in the way of young lovers; comic interludes provided by characters marked by their language as from a lower class; and humour created through double meanings and sexual innuendo.

Prose

This section does not deal with books that are compilations of material originally performed on stage, radio or television. (See Units 7 and 8.) Nor does it include books that are compilations of short, humorous extracts or comic novels. The term *comic novel* indicates that it will clearly be humorous, or satirical, in its *overall* purpose and structure.

HUMOUR IN CHARLES DICKENS

Other novels have humour occurring as one of many devices, alongside passages that have no humorous content. The novels of Charles Dickens, for example, have some richly comic characters, even though the work itself would not be classed as primarily humorous. Examples could be taken from almost any novel of Dickens. His characters are often described as 'caricatures', as their physical features and character traits are exaggerated to comic effect.

The targets of Dickens's **satire** in *Hard Times* are the utilitarian philosophies of education and industry, represented in the following extract by the character of Thomas Gradgrind. Dickens shows his ideals to be misguided, partly by the disasters that occur in the plot, and partly by individual scenes like this, parodying the characters and his beliefs.

Activity with text

Examine the techniques used to construct a satirical portrait of the speaker, Thomas Gradgrind, and all that he stands for. In what sense is it a caricature? Refer to parody of register, repetition and exaggeration; absurdities and incongruity; metaphor and simile, contrast and connotation.

Chapter 1 The One Thing Needful

'Now, what I want is, Facts. Teach these boys and girls nothing but Facts. Facts alone are wanted in life. Plant nothing else, and root out everything else. You can only form the minds of reasoning animals upon Facts: nothing else will ever be of service to them. This is the principle on which I bring up my own children, and this is the principle on which I bring up these children. Stick to Facts, sir!'

The scene was a plain, bare, monotonous vault of a schoolroom, and the speaker's square forefinger emphasised his observations by underscoring every sentence with a line on the schoolmaster's sleeve. The emphasis was helped by the speaker's square wall of a forehead, which had his eyebrows for its base, while his eyes found commodious cellerage in two dark caves, overshadowed by the wall. The emphasis was helped by the speaker's mouth, which was wide, thin and hard set. The emphasis was helped by the speaker's voice, which was inflexible, dry and dictatorial. The emphasis was helped by the speaker's hair, which bristled on the skirts of his bald head, a plantation of firs to keep the wind from its shining surface, all covered with knobs, like the crust of a plum pie, as if the head had scarcely warehouse-room for the hard facts stored inside. The speaker's obstinate carriage, square coat, square legs, square shoulders - nay, his very neckcloth, trained to take him by the throat with an unaccommodating grasp, like a stubborn fact, as it was - all helped the emphasis.

'In this life, we want nothing but facts, sir - nothing but facts!'

The speaker, and the schoolmaster, and the third grown person present, all backed a little, and swept with their eyes the inclined plane of little vessels then and there arranged in order, ready to have imperial gallons of facts poured into them until they were full to the brim ...

Chapter 2 Murdering the Innocents

... he seemed a kind of cannon loaded to the muzzle with facts, and prepared to blow them clean out of the regions of childhood at one discharge. He seemed a galvanising apparatus, too, charged with a grim, mechanical substitute for the tender young imaginations that were to be stormed away.

'Girl number twenty,' said Mr Gradgrind, squarely pointing with his square forefinger, 'I don't know that girl. Who is that girl?'

'Sissy Jupe, sir,' explained number twenty, blushing, standing up and curtseying.

'Sissy is not a name,' said Mr Gradgrind. 'Don't call yourself Sissy. Call yourself Cecilia.'

'It's father as calls me Sissy, sir,' returned the young girl, in a trembling voice, and with another curtsey.

'Then he has no business to do it,' said Mr Gradgrind. 'Tell him he mustn't. Cecilia Jupe. Let me see. What is your father?'

'He belongs to the horse-riding, if you please, sir.'

Mr Gradgrind frowned, and waved off the objectionable calling with his hand ...

... 'Very well, then. He is a veterinary surgeon, a farrier and horse-breaker. Give me your definition of a horse.'

(Sissy Jupe thrown into the greatest alarm by this demand.)

'Girl number twenty unable to define a horse!' said Mr Gradgrind, for the general behoof of all the little pitchers. 'Girl number twenty possessed of no facts, in reference to one of the commonest of animals! Some boy's definition of a horse. Bitzer, yours.'

... But, whereas the girl was so dark-eyed and dark-haired, that she seemed to receive a deeper and more lustrous colour from the sun when it shone upon her, the boy was so light-eyed and light-haired that the selfsame rays appeared to draw out of him what little colour he ever possessed. His cold eyes would hardly have been eyes ...

'Bitzer,' said Thomas Gradgrind. 'Your definition of a horse.'

'Quadruped. Graminivorous. Forty teeth, namely twenty four grinders, four eye-teeth, and twelve incisive. Sheds coat in the spring; in marshy countries, sheds hoofs too. Hoofs hard, but requiring to be shod with iron. Age known by marks in mouth.'

Commentary

The character of Gradgrind is constructed, both in appearance and speech style, as powerful, authoritarian and repressive type of man, yet he is made to seem absurd. This is done by parodying some recognisable traits of speech, but exaggerating them to emphasise the negative or ridiculous qualities. He repeats the word 'Facts'(the capital letter suggests it has the importance of a proper noun, like the name of an institution) more often than is needed (remember Grice's maxim of quantity – Unit 3). The structures are relatively plain and short and include a number of imperatives: 'Plant nothing else ... root out everything else.' He uses sentences that are noticeably shortened: 'Girl number twenty unable to define a horse.' This parodies the curt style associated with a blunt, plain-speaking man. He uses a number of absolute terms: 'nothing, alone, ever, only'. In the words of Ambrose Bierce, he is 'Positive at the top of his voice'. Though plain-speaking in terms of sentence structure, he uses a formal level of lexis: 'veterinary surgeon, farrier'. These terms are thrown into contrast with the words of Sissy Jupe, who had just referred to her father: 'he belongs to the horse-riding'. She has already been established as the likeable foil to Gradgrind and to the younger version, Bitzer, by the use of words with favourable connotations: 'a deeper and more lustrous colour from the sun'. In contrast, the words used to describe Gradgrind, his schoolroom and his favoured pupil have a negative range of connotations: 'vault', 'cellar', 'cannon' etc.

The narrator is also infected with Gradgrind's style of speech and repeats the word 'square' in almost every sentence. The sentence structure imitates the monotony to which he refers, by beginning a series with 'The emphasis was helped by ...'. This clumsy repetition helps to create a sense of irony, as the reader does not feel that anything is 'helped', rather 'hindered'. The absurdity of Gradgrind's views are highlighted in his statement 'Sissy is not a name', saying something which is patently not true (Grice's maxim of quality). He continues to refer to her as 'Girl number twenty' – using numbers not names has a range of aggressive or impersonal connotations.

Gradgrind himself is the butt of the humour, particularly in the physical descriptions linking the man to solid, inanimate objects. The caricature reaches its most absurd level when his head is compared, incongruously, to both a plantation of firs and a plum pie. The direction of the satire is widened out to embrace Facts, in the image of his 'neckcloth, trained to take him by the throat with an unaccommodating grasp, like a stubborn fact'. The absurdity of his view of knowledge is

81

shown in the contrasting attitudes to Sissy's and Bitzer's knowledge of horses: 'Girl number twenty possessed of no facts, in reference to one of the commonest of animals.' (It is her father's trade!) The desired answer is a wonderful exaggeration of a collection of incidental facts, expressed in abbreviated sentences with scientific jargon: 'Quadruped. Graminivorous. Forty teeth, namely twenty four grinders, four eye-teeth, and twelve incisive. Sheds coat in the spring; in marshy countries, sheds hoofs too. Hoofs hard, but requiring to be shod with iron. Age known by marks in mouth.'

HUMOUR IN JANE AUSTEN

The humour of Jane Austen is created through irony (see Unit 3) either in the author's voice or in one of the characters'. In the novel *Emma* Knightley's proposal of marriage to Emma is followed by this comment:

> What did she say? - Just what she ought, of course. A lady always does.

It is humour with a target - Austen's stance on the society of the time is detached and mocking. This, in turn, affects the reader's stance: 'he alone - reading between the lines - has become the secret friend of the author' (Patricia Meyer Spacks, 'Austen's Laughter', in Barreca 1988). It is not only in the author's direct comments that interpretation of the text is manipulated. The speech of the characters is sometimes constructed so that we do not take it at face value. In *Pride and Prejudice* Mr Bennet's response to his daughter's piano-playing is paradoxical:

> You have *delighted* us *long enough.*

Though a likeable character, his witty remarks are cynical:

> For what do we live, but to make sport of our neighbours, and laugh at them in our turn.

These passages are scattered throughout the text: in other words, irony is one of many narrative devices.

Patricia Meyer Spacks comments that there is a further way in which humour and laughter are used in Austen's novels to construct character and plot. The Bennet family are characterised partly by their laughter. In *Pride and Prejudice* the younger Bennet daughters, Lydia and

Kitty, laugh constantly and so reveal their triviality. 'Mary and Collins in their self aggrandising solemnities demonstrate their unawareness of a world outside themselves. Even Jane ... is a trifle boring in her relative lack of humour.'

Spacks points out 'the defensive function of both Mr Bennet's laughter and Elizabeth's - laughter which helps fend off real social, psychological, and familial difficulties.' When her father makes an insensitive comment about Darcy, she responds with a laugh, but

> Elizabeth had never been more at a loss to make her feelings appear what they were not. It was necessary to laugh, when she would rather have cried. Her father had most cruelly mortified her, by what he said of Mr Darcy's indifference.

Laughter cuts Elizabeth off from the possibility of romance and blinds her father to other people's feelings.

Extension

You have seen two examples of the way that humour can be used in novels. The variety of styles and purposes of humour in prose fiction is so wide that these two examples only scratch the surface (see also Sanger 1998). If you wish to investigate this area further, it would be best to choose a text that you find genuinely humorous and then use the framework outlined in Units 2, 3, 4 and 5 to provide a direction for your analysis.

Poetry

This section can also do no more than indicate a few examples of types of humour that are found in poetry. Sometimes the purpose is simply to entertain: there were examples in Units 2 and 3 that were jokes using the form of poetry. Sometimes the purpose is more 'serious' and the poetry may be termed 'satire'.

In this eighteenth-century extract, from 'Epistle to Doctor Arbuthnot', Alexander Pope produces a biting portait of the character Sporus. Although he has used an invented name, readers of the time would recognise his target as a living writer. As such, perhaps this type of humour should be termed 'lampoon', rather than satire. (A. refers to Dr Arbuthnot and P. to Pope.)

83

Let Sporus tremble – A. What, that thing of silk,
Sporus, that mere white curd of ass's milk?
Satire or sense, alas! can Sporus feel,
Who breaks a butterfly upon a wheel?
P. Yet let me flap this bug with gilded wings,
This painted child of dirt, that stinks and stings;
Whose buzz the witty and the fair annoys,
Yet wit ne'er tastes, and beauty ne'er enjoys:
So well-bred spaniels civilly delight
In mumbling of the game they dare not bite.
Eternal smiles his emptiness betray,
As shallow streams run dimpling all the way,
Whether in florid impotence he speaks,
And, as the prompter breathes, the puppet squeaks;
Or at the ear of Eve, familiar toad!
Half froth, half venom, spits himself abroad,
In puns, or politics, or tales, or lies,
Or spite, or smut, or rhymes, or blasphemies.

Sporus is described in animal imagery: 'this bug', 'well-bred spaniels', 'familiar toad'. The images have negative connotations and the point is given more force by the use of rhyming couplets and a neatly balanced structure: 'This painted child of dirt, that stinks and stings; / Whose buzz the witty and the fair annoys / Yet wit ne'er tastes, and beauty ne'er enjoys.' Sporus's surface pleasantries are captured in the image: 'Eternal smiles his emptiness betray, / As shallow streams run dimpling all the way.' Yet Pope is criticising Sporus's own tendency to destroy with words: 'Half froth, half venom, spits himself abroad, / In puns, or politics, or tales, or lies, / Or spite, or smut, or rhymes, or blasphemies.'

Activity with text

This modern poem by Adèle Geras – apparently a letter from Helen of Troy – may seem to be more innocuously humorous. Comment on how humour is created by the anachronistic register. Is there any target for the humour?

A Letter from Helen of Troy
Menelaus, darling
I do think this is all a bit excessive!
I can see you from the walls, you know,
don't think I can't,
beseiging away like mad, down on the plain.
Ye Gods, I thought, watch out, the gang's all here:
Hector and Agamemnon and Achilles
and that young man of his whose name escapes me,
the old bore, Nestor, even Ulysses.
I know why he's around. It's her, of course.
Penelope. Bloody needlework all day long.
He needs an outlet for his energy.
I do sympathise,
but still ...

I've heard the gossip.
Yes, even up here in good old Topless Towers
it reaches us,
don't think it doesn't.
That dreadful business with Iphigenia.
Well wind you asked for then
and wind you've got
and serve you right
and all for what?

I fancied Paris.
I would have got over it.
I've fancied other men before.
(You know that. I don't have to tell you.)
I think it was his thighs
like well-turned wood ...
but there you go ...
you cannot build
relationships on rippling flesh.
I've learned.
I'd have come back.

But you've overreacted as usual.
Now it's busy, busy, busy
hammering wood together all day long.
And what with that

and Cassandra moaning
and Hecuba criticising
and Priam losing his memory
and Paris going off me
on account of the fighting,
I'm bored to tears.

The rumour said a thousand ships.
I think war turns you on, Menelaus,
you and all the men.

It isn't about me at all.
Is it?

Commentary

The humour of the poem is based on the initial premise that Helen of Troy is writing a letter to Menelaus. We have to understand the allusions to the story in Homer's *Iliad*, that Helen – called by Marlowe 'the face that launched a thousand ships' – left her husband for Paris and so started the ten-year seige of Troy. There is dramatic irony in the gap between the reader's knowledge of the wooden horse they are building and Helen's ignorance of the trick that is about to end the war: 'hammering wood together all day long'. There is potential incongruity in portraying such famous characters as having the sort of emotions we would recognise – 'I do think this is all a bit excessive'; 'I fancied Paris. I would have got over it'; 'I'm bored to tears' – or perhaps it jolts us into recognising that humans remain basically the same across the centuries. Still the way we express our feelings today has certainly changed, so the concepts of modern therapy are amusingly anachronistic: 'he needs an outlet for his energy'; 'you cannot build relationships on rippling flesh'; 'You've overreacted as usual'. The incongruous register is maintained throughout the poem – the informal, spoken style of modern English, with fillers and tag questions: 'I can see you from the walls, you know, don't think I can't.' 'Well, wind you asked for then and wind you've got.' There is no attempt to create an archaic, or even a formal style, which we might find more appropriate for a historical or mythical character. Instead there are distinctive features of late twentieth-century English: 'Bloody needle-work'; 'serves you right'. It all creates a specific tone for Helen, so that we perceive her as a young, chatty female and the situation as no more momentous than everyday quarrels: 'beseiging away like mad'; 'but there you go . . .'; 'busy, busy, busy'. It builds up to a punchline, which hits with a serious point for the apparently playful joke about the situation being no more nor less than today's strife between men and women: 'I think war turns you on, Menelaus, / you and all the men. / It isn't about me at all. / Is it?'

Extension

Collect examples of poetry that you find humorous, for example poems by Wendy Cope or John Hegley. Try to categorise them. If it is satire – who or what is the target? What humorous devices are used – wordplay, parody, nonsense or the absurd?

seven

Spoken humour – television and radio

Television - and radio to a lesser extent - have replaced books as the main source of verbal entertainment. This means that a lot of contemporary humour is spoken and that you are more likely to watch and listen to humour than read it. Even though there are recordings, such humour is generally less permanent than written humour. The programmes that are popular in a given year may well disappear from popular culture within a matter of years. There are exceptions: some may be preserved on audio and video cassette, or be repeated. At the time of writing, *Monty Python*, for example, has become a comedy classic, but it is difficult to predict the current shows that will have a lasting popularity. This unit first surveys the different types of humour that are broadcast on radio and television, in order to guide your selection of suitable texts for analysis. There are two texts that indicate some of the different approaches needed. The activity hands over the choice of text to you. The framework of analysis established in Units 2-5·can be applied to any example of humour in language.

Radio

Radio is a good source of material for language analysis. It is important, first, to distinguish between the types of humour that occur.

On radio the spoken word is not supported by visual humour. In one sense, television has the advantage, but there are types of humour which can work only – or work best – in a purely spoken medium. The absence of a visual element allows ideas to work with the full range of the human imagination. The sci-fi comedy of *The Hitchhiker's Guide to the Galaxy* would have to waste money and time on special effects on television – although *Red Dwarf* manages to present a spaceship scene with economy. On radio the element of the unseen can be used to create laughs, as the listener (who cannot see what the characters can) follows one step behind. This device is rather like the element of misdirection in many jokes and riddles: 'Push her head between her knees' (Pause) 'Not that way!' (*The Glums*). The *Talking Head* monologues of Alan Bennet, although written for stage or screen, need little visual support: a single person is addressing an audience, rather than other characters. The radio monologues of Joyce Grenfell create the character of a nursery school teacher addressing children in her class – they are not seen or heard, yet the listener fills the gaps with their implied contributions. 'George, don't do that!' is the most famous running gag, with variations like 'George, what do Wise Men never do?' What he is doing is never made explicit. Bob Newhart also used the form of monologue where the implied contributions of the unheard participant create much of the humour, for example a telephone conversation with Walter Raleigh.

Within some radio programmes there are examples of ad-libbed humour, which may follow patterns similar to joking in conversation. Radio DJs on the music stations create a particular type of rapport with their listeners in the talk between records. This will reflect their personality to an extent, but it will be influenced more by the type of audience, Radio 1 catering for the tastes of a younger audience than Radio 2, for example. There is also spontaneous, ad-libbed humour on quiz programmes like *Just a Minute* and *Give Us a Clue* on Radio 4. (There are similar opportunities on television quiz shows like *Have I Got News for You*, and other game shows with celebrity guests like *Whose Line is it Anyway.*) The examples mentioned have survived for a number of years, but they are likely to be replaced by new formats. The humour in these shows often has a strong topical element, which quickly becomes dated; it also relies on familiarity with the participants and their relationship with each other – often adopted and exaggerated for humorous effect. This means that there are often 'in-jokes' and running gags, which also make the humour strongly context-bound and less easy to appreciate in a different time and culture. Although these shows are pre-recorded, there is usually a studio audience, so there is some overlap with the types of live spoken comedy examined in Unit 8. However, although though there is opportunity for spontaneous humour within the format (planned, if not tightly scripted) of these shows, there is less direct rapport with the live audience, as the programme is primarily aimed at the wider audience for whom it will be broadcast some time in the future.

This unit concentrates on forms of scripted humour. You should bear in mind that, of the five national radio stations, only Radio 4 and 5 produce significant amounts of scripted humour. Radio 4 unfortunately has such a limited audience - appealing mainly to middle-aged, middle-class listeners - that much new comedy is not heard by a wider audience until it breaks into television - and the best does so! (Alan Partridge, *Brass Eye, This is the Day, Hitchhiker's Guide to the Galaxy*, etc.). Although the quality is innovative, so that it should appeal to a wider and younger audience, examples will not be included here, because of lack of space.

Television

The examples in the activities have been drawn from television. There is a great variety of comedy on TV and it reaches a large audience, so it is potentially very influential. Television has a range of types of scripted humour, which can be summarised briefly to provide a guide for classifying and selecting examples for your own analysis.

SITUATION COMEDIES

Sitcoms have a series of weekly shows based around an initial idea of a situation and characters with potential for humour. These characters remain essentially the same, rather than developing as they would in comedy drama; (such examples would need to be examined within the context of other dramatic techniques). The humour in a sitcom comes from playing around with the comic possibilities of those particular character types interacting with each other in that situation, and may not involve lines or gags which are funny in isolation.

Analysis of the humour requires comment on the humorous potential of the situation itself, as well as examining individual occurrences of humour. (The entire transcript of an episode would provide too much data for close analysis.) For example, *Steptoe and Son* featured father and son rag and bone merchants; *The Good Life* followed neighbouring couples with different lifestyles. The type of situation perceived as funny will reflect preoccupations of that culture; perhaps the previous examples no longer have dramtic or humorous impact. Although British comedy has a high reputation and used to claim a higher degree of subtlety and irony, some of the most popular recent sitcoms are from the USA: *Roseanne* and *Friends*. It is interesting to note the type of situation which is perceived as having humorous potential for the society of the time. *Roseanne*, for example, was one of many American sitcoms featuring strong women as the central character; *Friends* inspired similar shows on British television, involving a group of young single people. Both shows reflect the move away from the nuclear family as the norm.

Only Fools and Horses ran for several series on BBC and its final episode was watched by a record 24.5 million people, so it indicates the current British taste in television humour. The situation is an extended family – two brothers living first with their grandad, then with their uncle in a high-rise council flat in East London. Both have aspirations to escape from their life-style: the older brother, Del, wheeling and dealing in anything which might sell on a market stall, the younger, Rodney, studying at night school. The title comes from the theme tune: 'Why do only fools and horses work?' Although this seems to be a critical comment on working-class culture, many of the episodes contrast the ethics of their way of life with yuppie lifestyles.

As well as the comic potential of the situation, the dialogue uses a number of humorous devices of incongruity. For example, there is humour in bizarre image: 'Poor old grandad – he was about as useful as a pair of sunglasses on a bloke with one ear.'

The discourse moves in unexpected ways, when the brothers are arguing about why Del wants to buy their council flat:

> Del: The flat has warm memories.
> Rodney: Why do you wanna buy it?
> Del: So I can sell it.

Still arguing about the flat, neat balance is used to create the twist in the punchline:

> Rodney: It's only fifteen minutes from the motorway . . .
> Del: And fifteen minutes from the ground!

The sitcom *Friends* has been so popular that in 1997 the series was re-run on Friday nights as the beginning of Channel 4's night of comedy advertised with the slogan 'Give your remote the night off.' A range of products has been marketed as a further mark of its cult status, so the material exists in a permanent form in videos and written compilations. The following activity asks you to consider the ways in which the situation, the characters and their relationships matches the definition (outlined on p. 91) of situation comedy, as opposed to comedy drama. More importantly, try to assess what makes this particular sitcom so popular.

You should have watched a number of espisodes of *Friends* to become familiar with the *set* features of the situation. For your analysis, select a single episode on video or in script form. (You can, if you choose, select a different sitcom and discuss a similar range of issues.) Although there are lines, or gags, within the show, which have features of incongruity with the *potential* for humour, you should concentrate on the *context* in which they occur in order to account for their humorous effect. Discuss the following questions. For questions 2, 3, 4 conduct a brief survey of viewers to find their reactions.

1. In what way is the situation itself conducive to the production of humour and laughter? Think about situations in which you are more likely to joke and laugh.
2. What is it about the *Friends'* situation that appeals to its audience?
3. What are the characteristics of each of the six main protagonists? Is it fair to say that they are each representatives of character types with humorous potential?
4. How do the characters relate to each other in pairs or smaller groups?
5. Find examples of gags for each character, or pair of characters. Is the type of humour distinguished according to that character or could the line be spoken by any?
6. What other characters are introduced into the situation? What comic potential do they generate?

1. The title of the sitcom points up a key factor: a group of friends hanging out together is a situation which is ideal for laughter and joking. Unlike, say, a meeting, there's usually no practical goal that the talk has to achieve; rather it's part of enjoying being yourself in the company of mutually appealing people. Knowing other people well means that talk need not be so explicit, but can rely on all sorts of shared knowledge and assumptions. Outsiders may well not share in the humour, as there's no intention to make the talk inclusive for a wider group.

2.   Yet this is a fictional and scripted scenario, so there is a need for an audience to share the humour. The most obvious target audience are those that can identify with the group of young, attractive, single New Yorkers, either because they share, or aspire to, those characteristics. The audience figures probably bear this out. There is vicarious pleasure in their successful life-style, marred only by minor setbacks. This description, however, suggests little more than the bland world of soap-powder adverts. The six protagonists are not simply glamorous, but have distinct character quirks.

3.   Here are a range of comments made by students about each of the characters:
Rachel: sexy, funky, dotty.
Monica: obsessive, competitive, obsessive about weight.
Phoebe: weird, new-agey, on another planet, unpredictable.
Chandler: witty, cynical, insecure.
Joey: over-confident, a lad, dopey.
Ross: sensitive, odd, geeky, introspective.
The sitcom thus features a range of personality types that occur in friendship groupings; they are good company, but can be infuriating.

4.   The situation from week to week explores all sorts of combinations of characters and the comic potential of the clashes: Joey and Chandler as flat-mates and rivals: Rachel and Ross with their on-off love affair; Ross and Monica with brother/sister tensions; Phoebe out on a limb.

5.   It would be interesting to test out written versions of the comic dialogue, without the speakers' names, to see how easily utterances could be matched up to the characters. Where the interchange leads up to a punchline, the 'feeder' lines could, perhaps, be spoken by any character, but the part which gains a laugh is often associated with a particular personality. Phoebe's comic lines, for example, could only be delivered by her. The humour is based on the oddness of her responses. The world she inhabits is one of high-minded aspirations, unaware of the need for a lighter, more trivial response in that situation: when asked what she wants for her birthday, she launches into deeply-felt wishes about her mother. She often interprets other people's questions and comments literally, ignoring the conventional force of the utterance: 'Guess who we saw today?' is a conversational opener that does not invite a protracted guessing game.

Ross's observations tend to delve so deeply into the implications of notions, for example 'if seven dog years equals one human year ...', that he loses the others – but not the viewing audience, who can laugh both at him and with him. Joey nearly always misses the point; he is a consistently good-natured but stupid fall-guy – literally in the scene where his soap opera character plunges down a lift shaft. Chandler is angst-ridden, but articulate and witty. He either sets himself up for a laugh with some lengthy soul-searching, or provides a devastatingly brief put-down. Rachel's character has developed from the spoilt rich girl who could refer vaguely to 'one of those job things' to a less easily definable character type. She is not so much a comic stereotype as a glamorous icon. Her love affair with Ross provides some romantic tension and poignant moments, though the saddest moments often generate some of the best jokes in an episode. Monica's character seems to generate the least humour – or popularity – perhaps because someone who is so sensible and organised is no fun. She tends to be the butt of humour.

6. Bringing in an older lover for Monica, with all the romantic implications of using the established 'heart-throb', Tom Selleck, added little humour, whereas other characters introduced into the series have had more obvious comic potential: the geeky new flat-mate for Chandler; his bizarre girlfriend, Janice; Marcel, the monkey, for Ross; the fat-ugly-naked guy. These characters add to the possibilities for running gags and in-jokes and thus the creation of humour which can only be fully appreciated by connoisseurs of the series.

TELEVISION SKETCHES

Apart from sitcoms, many comedy shows contain a series of different **sketches**, often with variations on a similar format each week. These may be presented by a single comedian, like Harry Enfield or Victoria Wood, or by a comedy duo, like Morecambe and Wise or French and Saunders, and occasionally by a team, as on *Monty Python* or *The Fast Show*. Each sketch will use distinct devices of humour and can be analysed as a free-standing text, though there may be a recurring style across the whole show.

Other shows create comic characters, who remain in character throughout: Peter Cook and Dudley Moore as Derek and Clive, Barry Humphries as Dame Edna Everage and Les Patterson. In this type of humour there will be the representation of a register appropriate for that character, but with some features distorted or exaggerated for comic effect.

Activity with text

Read the Peter Cook extract below. He is in character as Sir James Beauchamp, a High Court judge, being interviewed by Clive Anderson. First assess this created character. How would you describe Sir James, in terms of age, social background, personality? Now analyse his language – or rather the way his speech is scripted. What features of speech mark out his class and the formality of his profession? How does he trivialise his comments on the law, crimes etc.? How does he detach himself from the three deaths or accidents he mentions?

Look at the following markers of formality and informality: legal jargon versus colloquialisms; the choice of **intensifiers** (adverbs like 'very'); the use of the **passive voice**; and his inclusion of inappropriate details.

'Well, er, it's good to see you, judge. I say 'judge', because you're actually suspended at the moment, aren't you?'

'Yes, I'm temporarily, er, suspended for some mistake, er, judicial mistake, apparently I was deemed to have made.'

'Yes, being considered by an enquiry.'

'By - by - being considered by my peers and we should get the result very soon.'

'Yes.'

'It was an incident arising from a defendant being shot.'

'Yes.'

'In court.'

'By you.'

'By myself. It was a particularly unpleasant woman with specs, who was up on a charge of shoplifting.'

'Yes.'

'And I really became extremely irritated with her, because her testimony was obviously full of holes and completely untrue.'

'Yes.'

'And momentarily losing patience, I just vaulted over the dock and got her straight through the heart with a little Derringer I always carry with me in this pocket.'

. . .

'You've always had a strong sense of right and wrong.'

'I hanged a boy at school for, er, it was really dumb insolence, er, he was looking at me in that particular way, you know, irritating look and, er, when I say I hung him - or is it hanged - I never know which, well I strung him up.'

. . .

'There was a great deal of press comment about my jailing twelve people for life for, er, stealing some toffees.'

'Yes.'

'But that was not so much the crime that I jailed them for, it was the intent beyond the crime.'

'Yes.'

'Having stolen some toffees, in my view, though it was never proved.'

'Yes.'

'Having stolen the toffees, they then got into a first class carriage between Bristol and Plymouth and, er, started smoking.'

. . .

'Has any of this damaged you relationship with your wife at all?'

'Not really. My wife, as you know, is, er, slightly physically impaired, er, she had a - she fell off a horse - or was pushed off a horse. Nobody knows.'

'But you were there.'

'I thought she fell, but it's very hard to tell at that speed, going over those particular hedges with the barbed wire. But, er, a very nasty fall and she's partially paralysed down, down - one side is completely immobile. So she's very plucky, but I mean, you know, she can serve drinks, but not peanuts at the same time.'

Commentary

We hear a mixture of Judge Beauchamp's actual words and the sub-text: I am a respectable upper-class judge and completely innocent of any crime – or at least, unlikely to be caught for one murder and two attempted murders. I punish the riff-raff – whether they're innocent or not doesn't concern me.

He establishes his position of authority by the use of legal jargon; formal vocabulary such as 'deemed'; complex sentence structures and the use of the passive voice. Because he slips into everyday language such as 'specs', 'toffees', 'peanuts' within a more formal register, the effect is odd, and the effect of an authoritative voice slips. He uses a number of features associated with upper-class speech, such as his choice of intensifiers: 'particularly', 'extremely', 'obviously'. He sometimes uses the passive voice to avoid naming the agent, i.e. himself:

a defendant being shot = I shot the defendant
or was pushed off a horse = I pushed her off a horse

He mentions small details, which are innappropriate to the gravity of the situation that he is describing:

young woman - with specs

I hung him - or is it hanged? I never know which.

She can serve drinks, but not peanuts at the same time.

These features tend to parody upper-class speech for humorous effect, but there is also a cutting edge of satire, exposing the corruptness of the judge's power.

A further type of humour comes from **parody** of existing formats. In 1997 there were a number of parodies of the chat show format and their hosts: Alan Partridge, Mrs Merton. Occasionally the spoof is so close to the original that the participants are not aware that they are being used for humour, as in the apparent investigative/documentary programme *Brass Eye*. There are game shows that have lighthearted topics and use celebrity guests, but a recent development is the parody of the game show format itself: *Shooting Stars* hosted by Vic Reeves and Bob Mortimer.

Extension

Collect an example of humour from television or radio, and transcribe enough to provide data for your own analysis.

Stand-up comedy

In the 1990s stand-up has been called the 'rock and roll' of comedy. The comedians tend to be young, often male; they use the same venues as bands and attract similar audiences. Unit 7 also dealt with spoken humour, but there are significant differences between broadcast humour and stand-up comedy. Although there are examples of television and radio humour that are spontaneous and ad-libbed, the material is generally pre-recorded. This gives a form of protection, not only for the broadcasting company – mistakes, gaffes, offensive material can be edited out – but for the writers and performers. The material is carefully scripted and edited; the performance is rehearsed and may involve a cast of actors; it can be enhanced by a range of sophisticated effects; there can be several 'takes' before the final version is presented in its best form. Broadcast humour is not 'live' in the way that stand-up comedy is. This aspect affects the language of stand-up comedy in various ways.

Features of spontaneous speech

The first concerns features of speech as would occur in unscripted, informal talk. Although it may be scripted and rehearsed, the language must seem spontaneous. As well as use of colloquialisms, there will be more **fillers**, like 'sort of'; **ellipsis** (shortened forms of words); **redundancy**

and **back-tracking** (the repetition of words); and **sympathetic circularity**
- phrases like 'isn't that right?' addressed to the listener.

Activity with text

Identify the features of spontaneous speech in this extract from Lennie
Henry, as the character of Delbert Wilkins.

> I went to this club, right, and the bouncer on the door was typical, you
> know, big guy - he had 'hate' tattooed on one fist and 'fist' tattooed on
> the other fist. I walked towards him, I knew no fear, you know what I
> mean? - 'cos I'm from the Brixton posse, right? My hair was slicked
> back - my hair was so slick there was guys surfin' on it, you know what
> I mean? That's how slick my hair was, guy - I was feelin' mean - I was
> feelin' so mean I was refusing to lend money to myself. That's how
> mean I was feelin', guy. So I walked up to this geezer on the door, right, I
> said 'Step aside, Quasimodo - Delbert Wilkins has arrived!' And when I
> came to, this policeman was standin' over me saying, 'You're nicked,
> sonny.' And that's what we have to put up with in Brixton, all the time,
> right? Complete and utter hassle from the police, every single day.

Commentary

These are some of the features you should have picked out. (You may have
classified 'right' and 'you know' as either fillers or sympathetic
circularity.) Colloquialisms: 'hassle', 'So', 'this geezer', 'there was guys
surfin' on it'. Fillers: 'right', 'you know', 'so'. Ellipsis: ''cos', 'feelin''.
Redundancy: 'guy – I was feelin' mean', 'complete and utter', 'every
single', 'That's how mean I was feelin''. Sympathetic circularity: 'right',
'you know', 'you know what I mean?'

Effects of a live audience

Apart from these - possibly scripted and rehearsed - features of
spontaneous speech, any live act has to alter the text on the spot,

depending on how well it is being received: material can be inserted or removed; the order can be changed; timing can be speeded up or vice versa. Even when comedians take an act on tour, it is never exactly the same act. Some stick quite closely to the polished act, whereas others excel at the improvised material. It is, however, difficult to assess whether material is improvised on the spot, or simply appears to be.

There will also be features of conversation, because of the audience factor. Although comedy shows often take place before a studio audience, the cameras are the focus of the performance and the intended audience is removed in time and space. There is occasionally interaction with the studio audience, but heckling is virtually unknown – the audience seem to acknowledge their role as privileged to be invited guests. Every stand-up comedian has to take into account the possibility of heckling and be ready with 'put-downs': 'You're a good example of why some animals eat their young.' Even established, successful acts need to respond to positive audience reactions, and some actually rely on interaction with the audience to create some of their show.

Unlike other performances on a stage, the audience are not just the 'fourth wall' – present, but not acknowledged as present, in drama, for example. The solo stand-up comedian is addressing the audience, not other performers on the stage, and needs to build a rapport. This means that there may be conversational features as in one-to-one dialogue. The status relationship between the participants is different, however: the audience are generally addressed en masse and do not have an equal opportunity to take part. It is, in effect, a monologue, but with an implied, if silent, partner. Because the comedians are not usually creating a fictional context, they also have to respond to actual circumstances – unexpected noises like sirens or mobile phones.

Extension

Make a transcript of a piece of stand-up comedy on video and analyse it for features of spontaneous spoken language. Which of these could have been scripted in and rehearsed?

Confrontation with the audience

The 'naked' confrontation with an audience makes stand-up more dynamic, but is risky for the performer. The situation changes slightly if it is a double act: in this case, the comedians are interacting with each other primarily. There are relatively few female stand-up comedians. There are many factors around language and gender to be discussed - not least the myth that women have no sense of humour - but it is interesting to see how many women comedians prefer the double act format - French and Saunders, for example.

Other factors reduce the naked confrontation with the audience. Victoria Wood built her act around songs, and extended the sections of direct talk only when she was established, so that the songs became the filler, rather than the other way around. There is something reassuring about focusing attention on props, whether it is a piano or a book of poems. It is not only women who use props: comedians like John Hegley do not need to *read* the poems, but the book is there. (It is interesting that he refers to his wearing of glasses as a feature of his persona and act - is this a case of getting in first to sidestep any abuse?) The poems and songs, which are carefully scripted humour, also break up the stream of talk and reduce the stressful weight of a monologue, both for the speaker and for the audience. Some comedy acts, the late Tommy Cooper for example, are based around juggling or magic, which allow similar breaks in the focus. The visual aspects of the comedy cannot be covered in this book, but it is interesting to see whether this affects the type of humour used in the spoken interludes. They tend to be short gags, relying on ambiguities, which would seem corny if the entire weight of the performance rested on them:

> My wife. I always call her dear. She's got antlers sticking out of her head.

> I've got a sore head. (*Wearing a saw through head*)

Female comedians often use a character for their act. Caroline Aherne went on stage as the nun Sister Mary Immaculate, and later adopted the persona of Mrs Merton for a successful television series. This is Pauline Melville, in character as 'Edie'.

> I'm in the Women's Movement, you know. I am. I mean, I'm not in the most militant branch - I'm just in the branch that pulls faces behind men's backs ... My friend Eileen's had a horrible year ... She came into my kitchen in absolute floods of tears the other day - thirty years of marriage and she found out that her husband's a monetarist. I said, 'Listen, Eileen,' I said, 'sit down - I think all this monetarism's just a cry for help, you know.'

As well as being a vehicle for their humour, going on stage as a fictional character offers a degree of protection. Jo Brand used to suffer personal abuse from hecklers in the audience. She recalls one gig at Loughborough University where the audience were predominantly male and even a bouncer 'was heckling me, but it wasn't in a lighthearted way in any sense. It was really serious, really vicious. It was like being heckled by Peter Sutcliffe.'

Activity

List the comedians who are popular on the current stand-up circuit and categorise them according the degree of naked confrontation with the audience: are there props, the use of a persona etc? How many female comedians are there?

Alternative comedy

Comedy is risky, not only for the performers but for their targets. Laughter creates a bond between teller and tellee, and excludes the butt. The term 'alternative comedy' has been used since the 1980s to indicate a particular stance of humour. What is it an 'alternative' to? An old joke is that it was an alternative to comedy. It was, however, a rejection of the sexist and racist jokes that mainstream comedy had relied on. Tony Allen, the 'godfather' of alternative comedy, has this to say in his act.

> OK, stand-up comedy, I know what you want ... There was this drunk homosexual Pakistani squatter trade unionist takes my mother-in-law to an Irish restaurant, says to the West Indian waiter, 'Waiter, waiter, there's a racial stereotype in my soup.' No, no, no ... That's not to say I haven't got prejudices, 'cos I have. There's one minority group I loathe ... the Metropolitan Police Force.

The criticism is made by some that there is an element of po-faced preaching, which is not funny, but more importantly, that any 'political correctness' is a form of censorship. The comedians whom alternative comedy was reacting to, like Jim Davidson and Bernard Manning, insist that 'It's just a joke'. Yet in 1997 two Afro-Caribbean women won an appeal, claiming that their employers had failed to protect them from racial abuse and harassment. They were employed as waitresses at a function at which Bernard Manning made racially offensive remarks to them, encouraging members of his audience to join in the abuse.

Alexei Sayle explains why some targets are out of bounds for him: 'The important thing about racism is *oppression* – I won't do stuff about the Irish or women or blacks or Pakistanis because they are oppressed, and I don't want to make that oppression any greater.' This means that he might use jokes against a group he sees as powerful and oppressive, thus he would not object to jokes against the Royal Family. Most people set limits on the subjects of jokes: a fight broke out at the Comedy Store (a London club set up to provide a venue for an alternative type of comedy) after this example from Keith Allen, which pushed taboo subjects to the edge.

Bobby Sands [IRA hunger striker] says to Peter Sutcliffe [Yorkshire 'Ripper'], 'I bet I've had more hot dinners than you've had women.'

Activity with text

In its beginnings this comedy provided an alternative to the bland sitcoms on television. Its topics and language broke the usual limits imposed, creating 'dangerous comedy'. What features identify these extracts as alternative, rather than mainstream comedy? (No commentary follows this activity.)

1   I say, I say, I say – what's the difference between a pelican, the Inland Revenue and the South East Gas Board? They can all stick their bills up their arses. Why has Conservative Central Office got no toilets? Because everyone shits on everyone else. Hey, here's a cracker – what is the difference between a flock of Newfoundland geese and five hundred missiles homing in on London and the Home Counties? Answer, as far as the Fylingdales Early Warning System is concerned, there isn't any difference.

(Jim Barclay)

2   I've just been to New York and when I went through Immigration, they asked me if I was gay. I said, 'No, but I've slept with a lot of guys who are.' ... neither the British nor American governments will recognise AIDS as a disease. Now, that's strange because they both recognise homosexuality as a disease. If they think it's a disease, then if you're gay, don't go to work tomorrow – just ring in sick. 'What's wrong?' 'Still queer.' 'Hope you get better.' 'Hope I don't.'

(Simon Fanshawe)

3   When I was seven at school, one of my classmates told me that all Jewish people were wealthy. Nice one. You know, I remember that day, even now - running home excitedly to break the news to my mother and father. We spent that weekend taking up the floorboards.

(Arnold Brown)

4   All the time they keep stopping me - I say, 'Why?' They say, 'Suspicion.' I been stopped that many times I'm beginning to suspect *myself*. You know, I look in the mirror and go, 'Well, maybe I *did* do something, you know what I mean?

(Lenny Henry)

5   They fucking love me down the Arts Council, you know, down Piccadilly with the ponchos and the Lapsang Suchong, you know, and the trousers tucked into the boots, they say, 'Here's a working-class halfwit - let's patronise him!'

(Alexei Sayle)

Discussion

What type of comedy is popular in your social group? Is there now a backlash to the alternative comedy movement? Discuss the following three comedians' comments. (No commentary follows.)

Comedy is sort of incidental - it just happens that I've always made people laugh with my opinions. I do believe in change and I know you can change people. And I know that things are changing all the time. We changed the face of comedy to a certain extent - not very well; the original idea was to change the world, and to stop people doing Irish jokes, and mother-in-law jokes ... now people give lip service to that. He who follows the innovator does exactly the opposite of what the innovator does.

(Tony Allen)

105

Why is it that most comics can only do half an hour? It's because material comes from the heart. Irishmen are not stupid and it's not funny to say they are - you can pretend for ten minutes and then your cover's blown. Women's tits are not funny and it's not funny to say they are. So where do you look? You look around you, inside your heart and in what you're doing - that's where the comedy is. And inevitably that becomes social - you have to take a line.

(Ben Elton)

There was a traditional club comic got up at the Comedy Store and was racist and sexist, and anti-gay, and he just stormed. The audience might like me as well, but they would be quite happy to see Jim Davidson and Bernard Manning. You get a lot of bigoted and extremely reactionary people at the Comedy Store - and the abuse that women attract is quite horrifying. There's a whole male feeling which takes over, which I'd only really experienced when I went to see Roy Chubby Brown and there was a ninety percent male audience absolutely baying to hear the word 'cunt' said repeatedly.

(Jeremy Hardy)

Contemporary stand-up comedy

One of the most popular comedians of the 1990s is Eddie Izzard. He does not align himself with any particular movement in comedy. As he said, himself, about the material in his two hour solo shows: 'I just talk a load of bollocks about all the incredibly funny things in my brain.' Then he went on to introduce his first topic: 'Thimbles - they don't get enough press.'

Activity with text

Eddie Izzard rarely uses gags where the humour is based in wordplay; there is little reference to taboo topics and few obvious butts for his humour. Read the following transcript. (It would be better to watch a video to get a sense of his delivery.) What makes the audience laugh so much? There are aspects of incongruity, as discussed in Unit 3, and a sort of reversal of the superiority theory of humour (Unit 4), as much of the pleasure comes from a sense of *shared* experience between the teller and the tellee.

(*Talking about monsters*) They're big in our psyche. But you never actually meet any monsters - queuing in the corner shop for a Sherbet Dab.

Daleks - they were my favourite. But they were scary. I watched Doctor Who from behind the furniture. Didn't actually see any of it. I had to ask the dog. (*Mimes*)

Daleks had a death ray: 'We will exterminate. We are Daleks.'

And on the other side . . . a *plunger*?!

(*Voice of two Daleks, trying to come to terms with their weapons*)

'We will exterminate, unless we decide . . . ? Exterminate . . . or . . . ?'

'Why have we got this? It's a plunger.'

'You will die . . . or . . . ? Have you got any plumbing?'

'Death or plumbing. Death or plumbing.'

'Mainly plumbing? You've got a blocked sink?'

'Can you tip me up?'

Steve the Dalek has two death rays - he's very dangerous. Ken the Dalek has two *plungers*.

What did they have plungers for? They were never ever used. Perhaps they could walk up walls, but they only had one, so they just looked as if they were *about* to walk up a wall.

Sometimes they had a three-pronged claw. Like those you get at funfairs. There's a machine with lots of prizes at the bottom and you steer the claw down towards the furry bunny. It goes down and *feels* the bunny rabbit, and comes back with - absolutely nothing.

'We will exterminate, but now we will gather nuts.'

The Daleks had only one eye. They had loads of defects. Doctor Who spent years working out how to get the Daleks. His helpers were complete cretins. But it was easy. To defeat a Dalek, all you had to do is go up behind it and put your hand over its eye.

Daleks had another defect: They ran on wheels. (*Mimes chasing people*) 'Oh, they've all gone upstairs. Oh for fuck's sake!'

Then there was a later episode: 'Doctor Who and the Daleks go Upstairs.'

'Now we are all upstairs. Exterminate. Oh, they've all gone downstairs. Oh, for fuck's sake.'

And another thing: Daleks had wheels. You never see a Dalek chase across a shagpile carpet, or through the woods, or across a ploughed field. (*Mimes*) 'You're covering me in mud!'

Commentary

Eddie Izzard chooses topics that are trivial in a sense − fruit in supermarkets; queuing at a late-night garage shop; mowing the lawn − but the audience responds as he sheds light on the minute absurdities of the situation. There is a moment of surprise at the bizarre observations, immediately followed by recognition. 'What oft was thought, but ne'er so well expressed' (Pope). It's as if he wakes up some part of the brain that has been stifled by conventional ways of thinking.

He appeals to the audience to share the way he perceives the world. Rather than a burst of 'sudden glory' at the downfall of others (Hobbes's superiority theory − Unit 4), the laughter comes from delight in shared human experience. He chooses the familiar and commonplace, so no member of the audience is excluded. Of course, this is context-bound to the extent that you need to belong to a social group that watched *Doctor Who* in childhood.

This type of humour is sometimes called 'observational' − rather than witty one-liners, there is a gradual exploration of a situation and its absurdities. Like the cartoons of Gary Larson, strange images are created: the child hiding behind the sofa, asking the dog for updates on the plot. The cause of humour can partly be explained by the incongruity theory. Not only can dogs not talk, we do not think of animals as creatures with our interest in television plot. In Eddie Izzard's comedy the animal − and inanimate − world is credited with human properties.

His is a surreal vision, for example of pears in a fruit bowl resolutely remaining rock hard, till the people leave the room, when they rot. The audience laugh − now we come to think about it, what else can explain this observable fact about pears? The observations of the Daleks are absolutely accurate in their detail: the wheels, the death rays, the plungers and the three-pronged claws. First there is an element of surprise, as the audience had probably never really thought about them before. But there is the surreal slant of imagining these fictional creations as having the same thoughts and feelings as we do.

This challenges our assumptions about what non-human life is like. Names like 'Ken' and 'Steve' are not the sort of names we feel are appropriate for Daleks! It is strange to think of them having feelings of puzzlement and insecurity. It is also a convention that we do not require the same sort of logic for fiction, so a television audience would not normally think about a more sensible way to overcome the Daleks. We accept that there would be no dramatic plot if the heroes took the easy way out − and went upstairs, across a carpet or over a ploughed field. Eddie Izzard does not make one humorous observation and leave it; he draws out the original idea or analogy. And the analogy is often: suppose that animals or fictional characters worked to the same logic and conventions as humans, then this is how you would see the world.

Afterword

The aim of this book has been to offer a framework of analysis that can be applied to any example of humour in spoken or written language. Although a range of genres have been examined, only a few examples have been chosen from each and these examples have reflected the experience of the author. It should be possible to choose any humorous language data and conduct your own analysis using the approach suggested in the book. Try to find examples of current humour, whose appeal will probably lie in the innovative approach. Or look at genres that have not been covered: graffiti, strip cartoons, songs . . .

Much of the book has concentrated on humour in its social context. It's also important at a fundamental, personal level: as a way of bonding with friends, of coping with problems – 'You've got to laugh, haven't you?' – and of making sense of a world which sometimes seems to lack any. Spike Milligan was once asked about the comedy he writes: 'What were you trying to say?' He replied: 'Me.' (*Pause*) 'It was *me* coming out.'

index of terms

This is a form of combined glossary and index. Listed below are the key terms used in the book, together with brief definitions for the purpose of reference. The page reference normally takes you to the first use of the term in the book where it usually is shown in bold. In some cases, however, understanding of the term can be helped by exploring its uses in more than one place in the book and accordingly more than one page reference is given.

Not all terms used are glossed here, as a number of terms in the book receive extensive discussion and explanation in particular units. This is also by no means a full index of linguistic (and other) terms so it should be used in conjunction with other books, dictionaries and encyclopaedias which are indicated in the Bibliography.

acronym 14
A word composed of the initial letters of the name of something, e.g. RADAR.

adjunct 21
An element of clause structure, also referred to as adverbial, giving information about time, place or manner. For example, '*Slowly* the woman walked *into the courtroom.*' (see **clause analysis**).

allusion 4, 11, 47-48
Reference to something or someone outside the text itself.

ambiguity Unit 2
Words and structures that can be interpreted as having more than one meaning. For example, 'The students are revolting.'

anachronism 45
Linking a custom or event to a period to which it does not belong.

anagram 13
Re-ordering the letter of a word or name to make another. For

example, evil - veil - vile - live.

analogy 35
Referring to a partial similarity between two things or situations.

anaphoric reference see **reference**

antonyms 30
Two words whose meanings are virtually opposite.

back-tracking 99
A feature of spontaneous speech where an utterance is repeated in order to improve or correct it.

bathos 45
Lapse in mood from the elevated to the trivial.

bound morpheme 14, see **prefix** and **suffix**

butt Unit 4

cataphoric reference see **reference**

clause 21
A structural unit which is part of a **sentence** either as a main clause which can stand alone and be equivalent to a sentence

111

or as a subordinate or dependent clause. For example, 'The owner, who lives abroad, has written to all the neighbours' consists of a main clause 'The owner . . . has written to all the neighbours' and a subordinate clause 'who lives abroad'.

cliché 31
A phrase or saying used so often that it has lost its freshness.

collocation 18, 30
The way that terms are used and the words that tend to occur with them. For example, you would say 'dinner-lady' but not 'dinner-woman'.

comedy 75–76
A term used for a particular structure and plot in drama.

complement 21–22
An element of clause structure.

compound word 15
A word made from two others, e.g. 'newsagent'.

conceit 35
An extended metaphor.

connotation 18, 30
The connotations of a word are the associations it creates. For example, the connotations of December, mainly within British and North American culture, would be of 'cold', 'dark nights' and 'Christmas parties'. Connotations are often either individual or cultural.

contradiction 32, see **paradox** and **oxymoron**

conversational implicature 40–41; see Grice's maxims and speech act theory in Unit 3.

cooperative principle 40
Refers to the way in which most

conversations are conducted in a coherent manner with participants acting towards one another as efficiently and collaboratively as possible.

deixis 23–24
Words which refer backwards, forwards or extra-textually, e.g. 'that', 'here'.

discourse 9, 30, 41
A term used in linguistics to describe the rules and conventions underlying the use of language in extended stretches of text.

ellipsis 99
Ellipsis refers to the omission of part of a structure. It is normally used for reasons of economy and, in spoken discourse, can create a sense of informality. For example, in the sentence 'She went to the party and danced all night' the pronoun 'she' is ellipted from the second clause; in the dialogue

'You going to the party?'
'Might be'

the verb 'Are' and the pronoun 'I', respectively, are omitted with the ellipsis here creating a casual and informal tone.

filler 99
Words or sounds in spontaneous speech like 'er', 'sort of' that do not carry conventional meaning but allow time to think.

force 39
A term used in speech act theory to refer to the meaning something gains in its context.

free morpheme see **morphology**, 14–15
Unlike bound morphemes, these are free-standing words, like 'forget' in 'unforgettable'.

graphology 8, 12-14

The visual representation of language in writing.

headword 20

The key word in a phrase, for example 'a long, hot day in midsummer', where the other words are adding detail and description to the headword 'day'. See **modifier.**

homonyms 9, 17

Words spelt and pronounced the same, but with different meanings, e.g 'bark' (sound of dog), 'bark' (on tree).

homophones 9

Words which have the same pronunciation but different spellings and differ in meaning, e.g 'saw', 'sore'.

idiom 18

A sequence of words which functions as a single unit of meaning, e.g. 'over the moon' = 'happy'.

incongruity 7; Units 2 and 3

indirect object 21

Element of a clause.

innuendo Unit 5

A disguised reference, usually to a taboo subject.

intensifiers 95

Adverbs like 'very', 'awfully' used to modify adjectives - 'awfully hot'.

intertextuality 4, 37

The way in which one text echoes or refers to another text. For example, an advertisement which stated 'To be in Florida in winter or not to be in Florida in winter' would contain an intertextual reference to a key speech in Shakespeare's *Hamlet.*

intonation 10

The rising and falling tones in speech.

irony 50-51

A way of expressing meaning in language of a different tendency. 'Dramatic irony' is a literary technique in which the audience can perceive hidden meanings unknown to the characters.

lampoon 83

A type of satire mocking an individual.

lexis 8

The words or vocabulary of a language.

malapropism 11

Choosing a word with a similar sound, but inappropriate meaning. For example, 'Is it lunch time yet? I'm *ravishing.*'

metaphor 31, 35

A word or phrase which establishes a comparison or analogy between one object or idea and another. For example, 'I *demolished* his argument' contains a comparison between argument and war, also underlining the idea that arguments can be constructed like buildings.

modifier 20

A term used in noun phrase analysis.

morpheme 14

A morpheme is a basic unit of grammar in that it can function to mark a grammatical feature or structure. For example, 'walks' contains two morphemes: 'walk' and 's', the latter morpheme marking the tense and person of the basic or root morpheme 'walk'. Morphemes are normally divided into 'free' and 'bound' morphemes, the former occurring also as single words and the latter only occurring meaningfully when joined to the 'free' morpheme. Thus, 'unselfish' is a word made up from three morphemes, a 'free' morpheme 'self' and two bound morphemes 'un' and 'ish'.

Morphemes are often studied as inflectional or derivational forms: inflectional morphemes are morphemes such as 's' and 'ed' (bound morphemes) which indicate grammatical meanings; derivational morphemes are morphemes such as 'ship', 'dom' which can form specific grammatical categories - in these cases nouns such as 'friend*ship*' and 'king*dom*'.

morphology 8, 14-16
The structure of individual words in a language (see **morpheme**).

object 21
An element of a clause. For example, direct object e.g. 'She sent *a letter*.' Indirect object e.g. 'She sent *me* a letter.'

oxymoron 32
An apparent contradiction.

paradox 32
An apparent contradiction.

parody 47, 49-50
The mocking imitation of a person, text or genre.

passive voice 95
Shows that the subject in a sentence is the agent of the action or is affected by the action, e.g. 'Man is bitten by dog.'

phonology 8, 9-11
Study of the sounds of a language.

phrasal verb 17
A group of words with a single unit of meaning, e.g. 'put up with' = 'tolerate'.

polysemy 17
A semantic process by which certain words have several meanings, e.g. 'lap'.

pragmatics 30, 39
The study of language in use and the ways that sentences acquire meanings in contexts.

prefix 14
A bound morpheme like 'un-' attached to the beginning of the word 'unlikely'.

preposition 17
A class of word that normally precedes nouns to indicate position in time or space. For example, '*behind* the clock', '*before* Friday'.

pronoun 24
A class of words that can replace nouns, e.g. 'They [some students] were waiting.'

pun 8, Unit 2
A joke which relies on double meanings.

redundancy 99
A feature of spontaneous speech, where items are repeated even though this is normally unnecessary. For example, 'The *book*, that *book* I was reading ...'

reference 24
The act of referring to something. Anaphoric reference points backwards, e.g. the pronoun 'she' in the sentence 'I

saw the girl: she was wearing ...';
cataphoric reference points
forward, e.g. the word 'here' in
the following sentence. 'Here is
the nine o'clock news.'

register 30, 43

A term used to refer to the range
of styles or tones that can be
adopted according to the
situation, e.g. an 'informal
register' used when chatting to
friends.

satire 77, 83

The use of ridicule, irony,
sarcasm etc. to expose folly or
vice, or to lampoon an
individual.

self-reflexive 48

Alluding humorously to one's
own style. See also
intertextuality.

semantics 30

The study of meaning.

sense 39

A term used in speech act
theory referring to the meaning
of a structure, in isolation from
any context. (Contrast with
'force'.)

simile 35

The explicit comparison of one
thing with another. 'I wandered
lonely as a cloud.' (see
metaphor).

spoonerism 11

The transposing of initial
sounds of words.

stress 10

A term referring to the degrees
of emphasis given to syllables,
which can affect meaning, e.g.

the different stress given to the
verb 'present' and the noun
'present'.

subject 21

An element of a clause. For
example, '*She* sent me a letter.'

suffix 14

A 'bound morpheme' like '-ous'
attached to the end of a word
like 'marvellous' (see **prefix**).

surreal 36

Strange or bizarre.

sympathetic circularity 99

In spontaneous speech, appeals
to the listener like 'You know
what I mean?'

synonym 30

Words which have equivalent
meanings. For example, 'cheap'
and 'inexpensive'.

syntax 8, 23-24

The grammatical structure, or
order, of words.

tautology 32

A statement true by virtue of its
meaning alone.

tellee 57

The person or people reading or
listening to a joke.

teller 57

The person telling the joke.

tragedy 75-76

A term used to distinguish a
style and structure of drama.

transcontextualise 49, see
intertextuality

verb 21

An element of clause structure.

references

Barreca, R. ed. (1988) *Last Laughs: Perspectives on Women and Comedy* (Gordon & Breach, Amsterdam).

Blake, N. F. (1983) *Shakespeare's Language* (Macmillan, Basingstoke).

Chiaro, D. (1992) *The Language of Jokes* (Routledge, London).

Cook, W. (1994) *Ha, Bloody Ha - Comedians Talking* (Fourth Estate, London).

Crystal, D. (1987) *The Cambridge Encyclopedia of the English Language* (Cambridge University Press, Cambridge); revised edition 1995.

Driver, J. ed. (1995) *Funny Talk* (Do-Not Press, London).

Grice, P. (1975) 'Logic and conversation', in P. Cole and J. Morgan (eds) *Syntax and Semantics*, vol. 3, (Academic Press, New York).

Hutcheon, L. (1985) *A Theory of Parody* (Methuen, London).

Jacobson, H. (1997) *Seriously Funny: From the Ridiculous to the Sublime* (Viking Press).

Joos, M. (1961) *The Five Clocks* (Harcourt, Brace & World, New York).

Leech, G. (1974) *Semantics* (Penguin, Harmondsworth).

Merchant, M. (1972) *Comedy* (Methuen, London).

Morgan, F. ed. (1996) *Wicked; Women's Wit and Humour* (Virago, London).

Muecke, D. C. (1970) *Irony* (Methuen, London).

Nash, W. (1985) *The Language of Humour* (Longman, Harlow).

Pollard, A. (1970) *Satire* (Methuen, London).

Purdie, S. (1993) *Comedy: The Mastery of Discourse* (Harvester Wheatsheaf, Hemel Hempstead).

Rosengard, P. & Wilmut, R. (1989) *Didn't You Kill my Mother-in-law?* (Methuen, London).

Sanger, K. (1988) *The Language of Fiction* (Routledge, London).

Searle, J. (1969) *Speech Acts: An Essay in the Philosophy of Language* (Cambridge University Press, Cambridge).

Thompson, J.O. ed. (1982) *Monty Python, Complete and Utter Theory of the Grotesque* (BFI, London).

Wales, K. (1989) *A Dictionary of Stylistics* (Longman, Harlow).